CARE OF GAME MEAT and TROPHIES

Charles Elliott

Illustrated by
Douglas Allen Jr.

OUTDOOR LIFE BOOKS □ NEW YORK

Library of Congress Catalog Card Number: 74-33570
Funk & Wagnalls Hardcover Edition: ISBN 0-308-10206-1
                    Paperback Edition: ISBN 0-308-10207-X

Ninth Printing, 1980

Designed by Jeff Fitschen

Manufactured in the United States of America

To Jim Gay,
a delightful outdoor partner who has given me many
memorable days in the Wyoming wilderness

Contents

Trophy Room Ruminations

On the Wall of my den hangs the creditable head of a Dall sheep, taken in the far northern regions of the Yukon Territory. It is above average but lacks enough points to make the record books. Yet friends, acquaintances and casual callers look upon it with admiration and awe when I describe the land from whence it came.

Exactly what the rugged horns and wild pose stir up in the mind of the average fellow who studies this trophy I have no idea. Each fellow must envision something different. Some may behold only the sheep's head itself. Certainly no one sees in the trophy the same things I do.

To me that trophy is more than just an aging fixture on the wall. It recalls a wild mountainous land in Canada's far northwest Yukon. It elicits scenes of a rugged, isolated region, flowing with creeks and rivers the color and temperature of pale polar ice. It calls forth forests marching along the streams and climbing the hills before playing out as stunted pines in a desperate conflict with the arctic tree line. The pictures include tents pitched in the vastness of this unpeopled wilderness, a campfire that held back the chill of early fall, suns that circled the earth just above the serrated horizon, to dip out of sight only for a couple of short midnight hours.

I remember that month when we traveled through a world of our own, in which there were no signs of humans—only game trails and no manmade trails at all. Elsewhere in the world, the skies may have been crowded with air traffic. There we neither saw nor heard a plane for thirty days.

When I gaze upon that sheep head, I see other animals that we encountered—big burly moose with antlers of unbelievable proportions; bears that came to investigate the rattle of stones when our pack string slid down a graveled hillside into a creek bottom; great arctic wolves that moved along the far banks of the rivers and serenaded our campfires; the myriads of ptarmigans, ground squirrels and other small creatures.

None of these animals had any fear of man. It is doubtful that any we met had ever seen a human. We could walk close enough to touch many of

Here in his den amid trophies of a lifetime, author Charles Elliott turns outdoor experiences and savvy into the writing that has won him a large and loyal audience through the years.

them with a long fishing pole. The wild sheep were no exception. In all my previous experience, I couldn't get any nearer than the next mountain, if the sheep saw me first. Here, apparently, they had never been hunted. In a month's time, my guide and I climbed nineteen mountains for a closer look at rams to evaluate the trophy status of the heads. We were hunting on horses but, because the hillsides were covered with round, moss-coated boulders, we had to climb the mountains afoot. Most were so high and steep that we usually needed between six and eight hours to get close enough to study a head. Some sheep we passed up were magnificent animals, but we were trying to find a record.

When I look at that Dall sheep on my den wall, I don't see just the remains of an animal. Through my memory runs those rooftop slopes, covered with dwarf alders and willows and blueberry bushes loaded with luscious fruit as big as the end of a man's thumb. I see more than a score of rams, some of them we "walked" casually to within a hundred feet while they stood watching us curiously, probably wondering what manner of creature we were. I see seeps on the mountain top, to where we dug a couple of feet into permafrost for water. And I see unbelievable mountain vistas around us.

We turned down ram after ram, looking for that record of records, which we never found. Some of the heads were larger than the one we finally took. But in late August, with the snow line moving down the mountain each day, creating a background against which the sheep were becoming more difficult to spot and evaluate, we knew we'd better take a head or miss out altogether.

Although many years have passed since I took that sheep trophy, I recall every detail of the stalk. We spotted our ram so late that afternoon that a climb before dark would have been impossible. So instead of making the long ride back to camp, we bedded down in a clump of alders and willows. Since cold drizzle was falling, I expected a miserable night. Because our horses had spent much of the day grazing, we tied them in a protected part of the thicket and left the blankets and saddles on to help keep them warm.

The way the guides coaxed a fire out of that wet brush showed what manner of woodsmen they were. And they soon put a tarp up for a shelter while roaring flames dried our clothes. The guides then hung a healthy chunk of caribou ribs to broil beside the fire. We had packed the ribs along from our main camp. My dire prospects of cold, wet, miserable hours of darkness did not materialize, and that spike camp became one of my most enjoyable.

The next day, we found the ram near where we had seen it the afternoon before – on a lofty, narrow ridge that looked like a crosscut saw blade. Since there was no way to get our horses within a mile of rifle range, we hobbled them and left them to graze in the valley. Then on foot we made a long, circuitous approach up a creek bed that was bone dry on the surface but roared with an invisible torrent of water that cascaded over the permafrost several feet beneath us. We climbed the rooftop ridge and scratched our way up fifty feet to a position above the sheep. Then I lay for several minutes to steady my breathing.

At close range the head looked even better than it had through the glasses. When my .300 H&H Kennon Magnum cracked, the sheep pitched off that mountain as if trying to take flight and then tumbled end over end for more than a quarter of a mile down the ragged slope. If my bullet hadn't finished him, the fall would have. He was stone dead when we reached the spot.

Those are the scenes that come to mind when I look at that Dall head mounted on my den wall. My other trophies of bear, caribou, elk, mountain lion, antelope, moose and deer arouse similar sets of memories. These other trophies include heads and skins as well as other souvenirs owing credit to the guide's field know-how and the taxidermist's art in bringing parts such as scalp, skin, hoofs, and claws back to lifelike condition.

In the re-creation of something tangible between that moment you pull a trigger and those later years when you may recall every detail of the drama, the first and most important step is up to you or your guide. In the field, the makings of your trophy may be delicate and fragile, and unless they are treated with understanding and care, the trophy may never get mounted. Sometimes, even if the trophy is mounted, its life is often short, unless it has received knowledgeable handling. I am sure that every experienced hunter has lost potential trophies because the scalp or skin did not get the proper treatment.

Later in the book we'll examine how all trophies, whatever the size, should be handled in the field to make the job of the taxidermist easier and more effective.

In this connection, one of the most pitiful sights is the clumsy effort of an aspiring taxidermist to reassemble the antlers, scalp, and other parts of a mount when he knows little about the process. A deer is the most likely of any animal to get such treatment. I shudder when I see a creditable rack mounted with only about eight inches of neck behind it, instead of with the full shoulder mount that would have made it a beautiful trophy. Equally as bad is a neck that is long and skinny enough to remind you of a whooping crane. Too, it's upsetting to view a head with the scalp cut off correctly around the shoulders but with all the hair missing at the lips, nose, eyes or other spots; this missing hair shows that these areas were not cleared of flesh and thus this part of the hide spoiled.

On my library floor are five bear rugs. Three of these were prepared with the full head mount and are lovely specimens. The other two are headless—flat skins on a base of felt. The reason these last two don't have head mounts is that the guide either did not know enough to split and salt the fatty tissue around the lips, eyes, and ears, or did not take the time. He did a marvelous job of peeling the hide, of fleshing and drying it so that the skin as a whole came through in fine shape. But his lack of attention to the delicate areas, including the paws, brought a tearful letter from my favorite taxidermist. The writer said that the flesh had spoiled and the hair had slipped around those critical areas. Thus he advised against a full head mount. I can imagine how disturbing it would have been to lose a rug in this manner had it come off a world record bear.

Later in this book, I'll also give full instructions on how these bear skins should be processed to allow the taxidermist to re-create them as prized and magnificent trophies.

WHAT IS A TROPHY?

In my opinion, a trophy is any preserved memento upon which its owner places a high value. This value may be intangible, apart from what other hunters would consider a record, as with my white sheep from the far north Yukon. The hunter may place special value on the trophy because it was his first kill or his only one of a species. Or it may rank high up in the record book *North American Big Game,* compiled by the Boone and Crockett Club.

When a hunter fares forth into game country, he is after either meat or a trophy, or both. Though if he is an experienced woodsman, his choice of animal (or bird in some instances) often fails to meet the requirements of both categories. Seeking a trophy, the hunter will pass up younger and more tender-meated animals. But on the other hand, he knows how much meat he'll need for winter. For more than a third of a century, I did a lot of elk hunting in the western states. I've taken my share of the big animals. On my first trip, the only bull I wanted was one with a big rack. And since I was with Max Wilde, a famous western guide, I did get a creditable head, but it was nothing to excite the Boone and Crockett people.

After I'd taken a few bulls with outsized racks, I changed my tactics. First of all, I booked my hunts for no less than two weeks. Or if the hunts were with outfitters who set up ten-day packages, then I'd sign on for twenty days. Over many years I had learned that normally you just don't ride out of camp for a mile or two on the first day and knock over a world record head. The chances are that an average hunter will glass a lot of racks before he finds one that looks better than good to him. Then too, early in my western hunting, I learned the hard way. I'd taken a nice, average rack in the first couple of days, after which the guide and I devoted ourselves to looking for outsized mule deer.

One noon, after several days of deer hunting, we had stopped above a wide creek valley for our noon sandwich. While we ate, we glassed the country around us. Most animals are supposed to lie down in the middle of the day but not all of them are aware that they must follow this ritual.

Halfway through my sandwich, I noticed a movement on the hillside across the valley. I put my glasses on it and found myself looking at the biggest bull elk head I had ever dreamed of. I stuttered out the approximate location to the guide and he put his binoculars on the spot.

"Holy jumping cow! If that ain't a world record, I never saw one."

I'd already taken my elk. The guide had killed his earlier in the season. This meant that record or not, we were looking at an illegal bull. Believe me, I was tempted. To my knowledge I had never broken a game law, but at that moment I felt a strong desire to fracture one. We sat there watching the magnificent animal forage slowly out of sight beyond the contour of the ridge. Then and there, I made up my mind that on all future hunts I would devote myself to trophies. Failing to take a record-book trophy, I could, in the last few days of my hunt, concentrate on getting a good piece of meat.

This plan generally worked out well for me. I passed up many very large six-pointers which could have been considered in the trophy class. But I was consoled by the fact that I'd left them for other hunters who had never killed a big bull. Then along toward the last of the hunt, I'd usually get my winter's supply of meat.

On one occasion, when hunting with Anson Eddy in the Open Creek country just off the southeast corner of Wyoming's Yellowstone National Park, I came close to getting neither trophy nor meat. Anson was one of the best mountain men I'd ever known, and over the years I spent many delightful days with him in the mountain wilderness. He could trail a tumble bug over a rock slide. He worked out many a set of tracks that put us into position for good heads, most of which we didn't even try to get under our gun sights.

On this particular hunt we had passed up some interesting racks while looking for a record. We were approaching the end of the season, and also my hunting time was beginning to run out. We finally gave up the record idea and began to look for vittles. All along we'd seen young bulls, but now that we tried to find one, all male elk of every description seemed to have left the country. With only a couple of days left, I was getting a mite desperate.

On our last morning of the hunt, Eddy and I came on tracks which indicated a lone bull with half a dozen cows. They were traveling upwind, so stalking them was not too difficult. We caught up with the herd in a patch of heavy timber. The thick-beamed, slightly out-of-shape antlers indicated an old bull, but by this time I was not too choosy.

When I walked up to my kill, I knew that if it was winter meat I'd wanted, I'd made a mistake. His antlers told us he was an old bull and his teeth verified this. Tending to his cows and chasing away young antlered romancers had worn him down. I knew what kind of winter eating I was in for when I put my hand on his back and felt backbone under his hide. And I was right. I could have sold those steaks and chops for everlasting shoe soles and saved my teeth. So that bull did, in one sense, carry a trophy rack. I have never forgotten it.

ESTIMATING TROPHY QUALITY

To most hunters the word "trophy" usually means big or outstanding in one respect or another. Size is possibly the most important factor. One thing for certain: Even to a reasonably experienced eye, the bulk, the antlers or the horns always appear larger on a live animal than after that lethal chunk of lead has put it on the ground. The question is: *How can you judge the trophy proportions of antlers or of the animal itself, such as a bear or lion, before shooting?*

One of my favorite hunting companions over many years has been Jim Gay of Laramie, Wyoming. Jim served a long period with the original Jonas Brothers, who did much to raise the stature of real life taxidermy to its present day art. After World War II, Jim came back to Laramie and opened his own shop. Today, he is recognized as one of the foremost taxidermists anywhere.

His business is taxidermy but his first love is hunting. Each fall he turns his shop over to his wife, son and helpers and takes a job guiding for the pure and simple pleasure of being in the mountains and on the plains. Those clients who hunt with him have put many trophies in the record books.

Mule Deer

Until I first hunted with Jim, many years ago, my evaluation of a head was based only on how big it looked. I've downed many an animal that appeared so much smaller after I'd given it the coup de grace that I wished I'd let it go. Jim changed all this for me.

We were hunting on Platte Ridge, a 9,000-foot-high chunk of mountain between Platte River and Douglas Creek in southern Wyoming's Medicine Bow National Forest. With the guide, I came upon a brace of mule deer bucks standing in the jackpines, looking back at us. One of the bucks had a rack that, judged by whitetail standards in my home state of Georgia, made my old pumper skip a couple of beats. I started my .308 to my shoulder, but Jim shook his head. The bucks saw my movement and disappeared in a couple of bounds.

"Why didn't you let me shoot?" I panted.

"That's not the size trophy we're looking for," Jim replied.

"I guess you can tell from experience," I said, "but I'm just a run-of-the-mill mule deer hunter. How would I know?"

"By his ears," my partner said.

I stared at him and Jim chuckled.

"As a taxidermist," he explained, "I guess I do have an advantage. I've measured so many mule deer heads before mounting them, that I know all about the ears."

"What have the ears to do with it?" I wanted to know.

Jim's explanation gave me something I'd never heard or thought of in all my years of hunting, and it certainly is worth keeping in mind when trying to judge rack size under field conditions.

"From the white spot at the base of a mule deer's ear to the tip," he said, "is about eight inches. When he's standing and looking at you, the spread between the tips of his ears is usually 19 to 21 inches. A quick appraisal will give you the number and length of points on the antlers, the size of the brow points and—by comparing them with his ears—the length and spread of the antlers. If you judge the beams as three times the length of his ears, they're pretty sure to be 24 inches long or more—a good head. If the inside

Abnormal Point

Inside Spread

Abnormal Point

Even if you have a chance to view a head from different angles, it's tough to make a reliable estimate of trophy score by Boone and Crockett Club standards. But you can do pretty well, using these guidelines: On mature bucks, it's eight inches from the white spot at the base of the ear to the ear tip. In this photo, the general sweep of each antler appears to be three times the length of an ear—encouraging. Then consider that from erect ear tip to ear tip mature bucks measure 19 to 21 inches. This buck's widest inside spread of the main beams easily exceeds the ear tips and thus would be as ample as many in the records. But each main beam appears much less than triple an ear length, and thus short of the 24 inches which is common among top-ranking bucks. And since the sixth points on mule deer are considered abnormal, they here subtract from the score. Though an impressive head, the head of a lifetime for most hunters, this one would probably not qualify for the book.

spread extends outside the tips of his ears, then it's better than 20 inches. The farther the spread goes beyond those ear tips, the better the rack."

Jim went on to say that the depth of the chest from the withers to the bottom of the brisket usually runs 18 to 21 inches, providing another good comparison for the height of the rack.

Whitetail

In principle, judging antlers from known sizes elsewhere on the animal's body can be done reliably for every type of antlered game in North America.

Each year more whitetail deer are bagged than any other hoofed game animal. Ranging over a sizeable portion of the continent, the whitetail comes in a number of recognized species, and often the size of the animal depends on its location. The Florida Key deer, for instance (which is protected), seldom weighs more than 80 pounds. The carcass of the largest whitetail on record is said to have weighed around 425 pounds.

Naturally the smaller animal is equipped with smaller accessories, and on one subspecies the ear length and spread may be different than on the next.

The deer in my home state of Georgia may be considered about average, so I asked Ken Willis, my butcher, to measure a number of the bucks brought in for skinning and processing. He found the average length of the ears to run between 6 and 6½ inches and the average spread between the ear tips to be around 13 to 14 inches. These measurements are a bit smaller than those from the mule deer, but they give the same basis for comparison with antler size.

Tough, quick shots are often the rule for whitetails. If each main beam runs four times the length of an ear, the beam will measure 24 to 26 inches—a rough, average minimum for record class deer. The inside spread should extend at least a few inches beyond each of the ear tips. Then uniformity of long corresponding tines (at least five to a side) and massiveness add to the score. With an inch or two more on each of the tines and in the spread, the buck in this photo would probably make the book.

As an example, the Boone and Crockett Club minimum requirement for the whitetail is 170 points. This covers several features of the antlers, but the average length of the main beam among the eleven smallest heads shown in the book runs about 25 inches. This means that if that quick evaluation you give an old trophy whitetail shows that each main beam is four times or more the length of an ear, you may be looking at a buck in the record class.

But look at other features too, including the massiveness of the antlers, the number of points, the length of the brow points and the width the rack extends beyond the ear tips. Ken's measurements show the distance between the tops of the ears in their natural position of attention as $12\frac{1}{2}$ to 14 inches. If the inside spread of the rack extends several inches beyond the ear tips on each side, and other features are outstanding, the chances are that you'll bag a trophy that's a good candidate for the steel tapes. The world record whitetail had an inside spread of only $20\frac{1}{8}$ inches, but the rack was high and massive otherwise.

Pronghorn

On my den wall is what I think is a reasonably good antelope head. It doesn't quite make the minimum requirements for entry in Boone and Crockett Club records, but I couldn't be more proud of it if it were high in the book, since it was my first pronghorn, taken many years ago. The guide and I didn't stop to evaluate the head in terms of Boone and Crockett. All we knew was that in comparison to others we had seen, it was a trophy worth trying for.

Later at home and taking a cue from Jim Gay, I made some measurements of the mounted head. This I did partly out of curiosity and partly because I thought an evaluation would help were I to hunt the pronghorn again. I didn't make those measurements necessary to score the head properly. I made only those which I thought might help me in the field: the distance from the tip of the nose to the base of the horns; the space between the tips of the ears; the length of the ears; the height of the prong; and so on. This, I figured, would help me pick out a prize rack.

When I told Jim Gay what I had in mind, he said, "All this comparison takes time, and for antelope I have sorta developed a quick-at-a-glance way from profile points of reference, easy to see from a distance. Where does the tip of the ear, when erect, come in relation to the prong? For a good buck it usually comes only up about halfway to the prong. The horn above the prong should be equal to the distance from the base to the prong.

"After you evaluate those two points, look at the amount of curve – the more the better, as this really seems to add points. It's eight inches from the eye to the end of the nose, so if this distance equals that from the *base to the*

Though this alarmed pronghorn (note flared rump patch) is a fairly ordinary buck, the photo illustrates useful head features for field estimation. Consider that an ear runs about four inches and that the distance from nose tip to eye is about eight inches. Since the outside curve of each horn on record heads usually measures 16 inches or better, you can use four ear lengths or two nose-to-eye distances as comparison. The horns on this buck run far short short of 16 inches. Other key measurements include circumferences of horns and lengths of prongs — in this photo not exceptional. Horn conformation does not affect the score.

prong, with that much (about eight inches) of horn above the prong, chances are you'll have a trophy that makes the book — if you can get him.

"The eye is located right at the base of the horn, and is even with the base of the ear. So the eye makes a good pivot point. Looking at the horn alone, you can get fooled."

Extra Point

3rd Point
Hidden by 2nd

Lengths of main beams on high-ranking elk trophies approach five feet. And hoof to withers, big bulls measure about five feet. Thus comparing this body dimension with the main beams helps in making a quick, rough assessment. Other factors include uniform lengths of corresponding points, massiveness and inside spread. The fine, mature bull in this photo has six points on his right antler and seven on his left—the second point hiding the third. The extra point would be classed as normal, neither adding to nor detracting from the total score.

The author killed this fine Alaskan Dall long ago. Posed with the head is Lou Minear, a hunting partner. For sheep, official score is based only on the length of each horn's outer curve and four circumferences en route. Record-book horns show a full curl, as these show. Unfortunately, the author gave this head away before the establishment of Boone and Crockett standards for measurement. Though many hunters like a wide tip-to-tip spread, it does not directly affect the score.

Elk

Since there are so many measurements to take into consideration, an animal of the big-antlered variety may be a bit more difficult to evaluate. An elk, for instance, has six, sometimes seven and rarely more points on its massive rack. The length and circumference of all these count in the scoring, and any abnormal points must be subtracted from the total score. Other important measurements are the lengths of the main beams and extent of the greatest inside spread. Since you can't walk up to an old bull and measure with your tape or yardstick, and sometimes have to make these evaluations in a hurry, a good rule of thumb is shoulder height above the ground. The withers of a big animal may be as high as five feet, and if the length of each antler beam approaches hoof-to-withers dimension, the chances are that you've got yourself a real trophy.

Dall Sheep

The few times I hunted Dall sheep in Alaska and in the Yukon Territory, we went largely on spread from tip to tip. As a rule, at that point where a Dall's horns have made about one full curl, the tips begin to spiral outward, away from the head. Generally the greater the distance between the points, the better the head — especially if the base is massive. But the important scoring measurements for sheep are various circumferences of the horns as well as lengths around the outside curves.

Caribou and Moose

Naturally, because of the shape of its antlers or horns, each of the hoofed animals is judged by a different set of standards. Width of the brow and top palms count for caribou. Both width and length of palms are big factors in evaluating the moose.

Dangerous Carnivores

The record fur animals, as the bears and cats, are determined by the length and breadth of the skull. Taking the skull measurements of a jaguar or grizzly before shooting it is not the healthiest chore I can think of. Thus most of the guides and hunters judge these game animals — usually from a distance — by overall size. A nine-foot Kodiak bear is likely to have a larger skull than a bear two-thirds as large. If that smaller bruin is the first you've ever seen, he'll look as though he is twelve feet tall and weighs a ton. It's best to go by the judgment of your guide. One thing you both want to be sure of is that the bruin is not wearing his summer coat of thin and worn or mangy-appearing fur. He grows his thick winter coat before hibernation and is still wearing it when he comes out in the spring.

Pictured here are a cougar, a silvertip grizzly, a black bear, and a brown bear mouthing his lunch. For bears and cats, skull measurements (official) and condition of fur (personal) are the chief trophy considerations. Big animals have big heads. But regarding size, the author recommends relying on the estimate of an experienced guide whose heart may not be booming as powerfully as yours.

Color in the selection of a rug may be a factor. I've known gunners to pass up an ebon black bear because they wanted the brown phase of this same species. And a real old silvertip is more to be desired than one darker in color, which usually marks a younger grizzly.

Color accounted for one of my disappointments on a hunt to a northern corner of the Yukon. Our outfitter, Louis Brown, told me of a grizzly he'd come across in those parts. Its full coat was a lighter brown than that carried by most grizzlies, and it wore a golden saddle just behind its massive shoulders. As far as I knew, this could have been an undiscovered subspecies or just an unusual marking on one individual in that isolated corner of the world.

I saw the bear, whatever it was. Paul Germain, my Indian guide, and I were riding up a creek valley when the grizzly boiled out of a thicket in front of us. I had only half believed Louie's story and even now could scarcely credit my eyes. The grizzly was a lighter russet than most I'd seen, and there was a definite golden stripe across its shoulders. I peeled off my horse and drew my rifle out of the saddle scabbard with the speed of a gun slinger of the old West. I didn't use the gun though. Two cubs bounced out of the thicket behind the unusual grizzly, and of course no one shoots a mamma bear. If this fur was only in a color phase, it was the only one of its kind in our encounters. And it made for the most beautiful bruin skin I ever saw.

GOING FOR MEAT

As for bear meat, I'm not keen on it. The big Alaska brownies feed on fish. Thus when you skin one out, it's likely to smell like a three-week-old mackerel too long in the hot sun. In the spring many grizzlies – and blacks too – feed on carrion of wounded game animals or winter-killed stock. In the early fall I've killed young blacks far back in the mountains, where they had been feasting on berries, insects, rodents and such. A chunk of meat from such a bruin, roasted slowly over the campfire, is worth sinking a tooth into. When you skin a bear, the smell will usually tell you whether you want to try a piece of it on a spit.

Mostly we kill hoofed animals for food. After listening to opinions over many years, I have about come to the conclusion that no one is neutral on the subject of wild meat. They either relish it with enthusiasm or despise it altogether. Those who don't like wild meat often don't know why. But you can be almost certain the dislike has resulted from an attempt to eat tough meat from an old, lean bull or from errors in the processing of the animal from the moment it hit the ground.

Usually considered less important than the trophy, game meat has gone to waste in colossal amounts because it was not handled properly in the field. All of this will be discussed more fully in a later chapter. Suffice to say that wild meat, cared for from the moment of the kill and put through the proper processes all the way to the table, is more flavorful and tasty than that from force-fed domestic animals. This rule is true also regarding meat of fish, such as trout, taken from wild streams as compared to meat from trout raised in hatcheries or rearing ponds.

Our nation grew up on wild meat, and in these modern times literally thousands of Americans depend on it as a substantial part of their diet. But most of these people know how to process and preserve the meat. For those who do not, this book will show them how.

Trophy hunting and meat hunting are different in some respects. When you are after a record head, you may pass up dozens of animals which do not meet your specifications and, in fact, you may never take a head of any description. Once I hunted Arizona's Kaibab with two hunters who were determined to get their names in the record book. At that time the area was overrun with what I considered excellent racks, and I collected one of them. But its measurements didn't add up to a record. We were there for a week and neither of those guys pulled a trigger. They stuck with the trophy idea right up to the last minute of the last day.

What I look for when I go after meat is a reasonably young animal, such as a forked-horn buck or a spike buck where it's legal. Or I may go after an elk of four or five points or less, with a broad rump or saddle. Then too I may take a doe or cow or other animal that looks to be good eating. Some of my western buddies who take their winter's meat out of the elk herd prefer a "dry" cow — one that hasn't been bred. They can spot such a cow and try to point it out to me. These cows are darker in color, and they are fatter and sleeker than the others. I nod in solemn agreement. But since I have never been able to see the difference, when I'm out for meat, I take a young bull.

The activity of any animal must have a lot to do with its eating qualities. A deer on starvation rations, regardless of age, won't be much good. And a buck that has been run before a pack of hounds usually yields meat that is tough and strong. Deer hunting with dogs is a southern tradition dating back to colonial days and continues today along the coast and in the coastal plains of some of the southern states where the swamps and thickets are so dense that without hounds to help in the harvest, many bucks would die of old age. This type of hunt is more in the character of a party, with gunners placed on stands and a dog pack and handlers driving the thickets. A fellowship get-together and barbecue usually follows the hunt.

On one of these hunts I had occasion to learn how the meat of a deer is affected when the animal makes a long run before the pack. We heard the dogs strike and for an hour listened to the deer circle and dodge back and forth through the palmettoes and gallberries, before it tried a straightaway course. Near where I stood, a fence ran along the country road, and the buck headed for that. The fence was only five feet high and normally any deer could have cleared it with almost five feet to spare. This buck apparently had run itself down. Its front feet hit the top strand and he spilled over into the edge of the road, landed on his head and broke his neck.

Ward Rosier, another hunter nearby, and I went to the dying buck. It was a young forked-horn, fat, and should have made a palatable chunk of meat. As is the custom in those parts, Ward put his hunting knife in at the base of the neck and cut the jugular vein to bleed the deer. In a few minutes it was stone dead. "Stone" is the correct word. The buck's muscles from the long run stiffened up immediately until they were almost as hard as rock. We field-dressed the deer on the spot and less than a quarter hour later hung it in camp to complete the job of skinning and cutting up the carcass. It was almost like dissecting a pine knot. Ward shook his head.

"We'll never be able to chew this critter, and if we could, we'd never digest it."

Wisely, he put the meat through a meat grinder with a like amount of pork and made sausage out of the entire deer, and even then I thought some of that sausage tasted a bit rubbery.

I pass up any meat animal after the rutting period, especially where he's had to fight off other zealous younger bucks or bulls between the times he's been busy with his domestic chores. Frankie Lasiter, one of my western guides, and I once lay on our bellies in the edge of a meadow and watched a poor old bull try to tend a dozen cows while four younger swains hung around the outskirts of the harem. Some of the cows were inclined to cooperate with the ardent young bulls, and the herd papa was one of the most harassed and exasperated individuals I ever saw of any species. He had worn himself thin and we passed him up, although he carried a good rack.

Key scoring factors for moose are number of normal points as well as length and width of palms. The outsized rack shown here with Yukon guide Bill Boone came from a fat old bull taken by a member of the author's hunting party before the establishment of Boone and Crockett standards. It is not known whether the rack was ever officially measured. Here the difference between the widths of the right and left palms would be subtracted from the score.

In contrast we once bagged an old bull moose in northwest Canada. The signs indicated that he had been living all summer in quarters as comfortable as I suppose a moose can have. The entire mountainside was crowded with willows and alders so that his food supply was more than adequate. A thick-crowned clump of spruce provided shade, and under this cover he had dug himself a bathtub with a good supply of spring water. Apparently he had loafed there since the snow had gone off the mountain, for although he was a huge bull with a spread of almost seventy inches, the layers of fat throughout his body were as thick as I ever saw them on a black angus steer. The old rascal carried a hunk of tender meat, too. The day we killed him, we broiled steaks over the campfire. They were juicy, sweet and tender enough to cut with a fork. It certainly revised the opinion I had packed around for long years that all moose meat is held together with rawhide shoelaces that would strain the ivories and strong jaws of a husky dog.

With most game animals smaller than moose, such as elk and deer, and birds, too, getting tender meat is a matter of pot luck. You can't size up a rabbit darting through the brush in front of you, and it's rather difficult to evaluate a teal barreling over your decoys at over sixty miles per hour. A possible exception to this is the wild turkey gobbler. You can usually tell his approximate age by the size and length of his beard, but out of at least a hundred devout turkey hunters I know, there's not a one who wouldn't pass up a young tom to down an old patriarch with a long beard and sharp spurs, no matter how tough they thought the meat of the old gobbler might be.

There is, of course, more latitude in treating feathered game. And there are several schools of thought on how it should be handled in the field. I hunt with people who gut every creature as soon as it hits the ground. I have other friends who believe that large feathered game should be hung by the tail feathers until the carcass pulls loose from them, at which time it will be "ripe," and I heartily agree that by this time it will be. Others say that small game birds can be frozen — feathers, entrails and all — until they are ready to be cleaned for the frying pan or pot, and that this makes them more tasty.

The surest way to preserve one of the smaller creatures for the taxidermist is to freeze it whole and deliver it to him in this condition. With birds handled thus, it is desirable to keep the feathers as neatly in place as possible. On rare occasions, when the specimen is valuable enough and no freezing facilities are available, a bird may be skinned. But generally this is a job for the experts and requires considerable skill.

All of the methods of preserving both the meat and skins of smaller animals and birds, as well as fish, will be discussed more fully later in the book.

2

The Kill

YOU HAVE DECIDED on the animal or bird you want for a trophy or for meat, or for both. You've made a successful stalk or wait, and the best shot you were capable of making. Your game lies on the ground in front of you. Now, it seems, all you need do to complete the job is field-dress the animal if it's big, or perhaps pick it up and put it in your game bag if it happens to be a quail, rabbit, duck or one of the smaller species.

Whether it's large or little, the very best bit of advice anyone can give you is to make certain the animal or bird is dead before you put your gun aside and get too close. This is not as likely to apply to small game as to the larger animals. But I had one friend who came home with several doves and deposited them temporarily in the refrigerator until he could get around to cleaning them. When his wife opened the refrigerator door, one of the doves was sitting on a shelf. It flew out past her and then through the open back door.

At a young but not too tender an age, I received a couple of lessons I've never forgotten on taking liberties with half-killed game. The first incident involved a gray squirrel. I shot it out of a tree top, and it hit the ground almost at my feet. When I reached over to pick it up, the squirrel jumped from under my hand and started for the hollow at the base of the tree. I simply wasn't going to let that gray get away. I caught the hind end of his body just as he got into the opening of the hollow. It took me about three seconds to pull him out and three minutes of trying to turn him loose. I never had my hands so full of anything that didn't want to let go. When I finally did get him shook off, he had no more interference about going into that hollow. My hands looked as though they'd been in a slapping contest with a wildcat. Never since that moment have I picked a squirrel off the ground until I knew it had journeyed beyond rigor mortis.

My other such affair was with the larger version of the Canada goose. Two big flocks came south each fall and spent the winter on Jackson Lake, near my home town in middle Georgia. I was in my teens and bagging one of those old honkers was the biggest ambition of my life. Almost the entire season went by before I succeeded. The geese would spend the night on the lake and after sunup fly to one of the many cornfields in the vicinity. They seldom went back to the same cornfield more than twice in succession, and it was purely a matter of guessing which one they might come to. Many a morning I slowly congealed against the frozen ground on which ice was spewed up all around me and waited for geese that never came. The few times a flock did show, it seemed invariably to light in another section of our field, and I could never get close enough for a shot.

Then one morning my luck broke for the better. I was partially hidden from the icy wind in a clay wash that ran through the cornfield and had about decided that I couldn't take it any longer when I heard the call of the geese and saw that wavering line come over the tree tops along the river. The field was extra large and ran around a rolling hilltop. I expected to be bypassed again. Instead the flock came directly over me. They were a bit high, and I led the old gander in front by a good ten feet. But my shot string apparently only shook him up enough to make him slide sideways and while the remaining birds fought for altitude, he glided toward the river, about three hundred yards away. He got only half way there before he touched down and started afoot for the river.

In my youthful exuberance and inexperience, I laid my gun on the ground and took off after him. It never occurred to me that the gun might shoot again. I caught the big gander before it got to the river, and within the next few minutes took the worst beating I've ever had from man or beast. That bird must have been the heavyweight champion of his species. He threw punches with the elbows of his wings that staggered me like a left hook. And while I was trying to get my arms around his wings and hold them down, he came near scalping me with his bill.

I finally subdued him before I was peeled and battered to exhaustion. When I had him all wrapped up in my arms, I didn't know what to do with him except to go back to my gun, turn him loose and shoot him again. But I didn't. I brought my goose home alive, put him in a pen and fed him until whatever wounds he had, completely healed. When I turned him free again in sight of his flock, resting in the middle of the broad waters of Jackson Lake, he flew to rejoin the others and probably to recount his championship battle.

I'm thankful that I learned my lesson on small game. Thereafter I knew how foolish it would be to take for granted that any creature I shot was dead or so badly hurt that I wouldn't be in danger. It may be that the older a fellow gets the more cautious he is, or it's possible that the careless hunters don't grow old. Few experienced guides or gunners will approach a carcass that appears lifeless without having a gun loaded and ready.

Not long ago I shot a buck with my .50 caliber muzzle loader. The deer
went down and sprawled out and appeared dead. I'm too old a hand to run
up, lean my gun against a tree, whip out my hunting knife and start carv-
ing. I reloaded that flintlock as quickly as my twelve thumbs would allow,
but in the process I probably spilled more than my usual amount of powder
on the ground. I had no idea whether I'd need that second bullet, but if I
did, I knew it would be much more effective in the gun barrel than in my
pocket.

If I hadn't stopped to load, I'd have lost my buck. As I came down the hill
toward him, he jumped to his feet as though he had been only momentarily
stunned. I put the second ball between his shoulders, breaking his back.

I'm sure that the caution I started developing in my squirrel and goose
days once saved my life in Alaska. We were hunting in the Talkeetna
Mountains above Anchorage and had taken a number of good trophies.
Since the weather was unseasonably warm, our guides decided that if we
wanted to save the meat, they would have to spend two or three days packing it into the ice house at Palmer.

While they were away, I spotted a grizzly grazing on blueberries on a
high hillside across the valley. I decided to try for it. The horse wrangler,
who also had a guide's license, and a fellow hunter accompanied me. That
horse wrangler was Johnny Luster, who later became one of Alaska's
famous guides and established his own outfit. On this occasion Johnny did
not pack along his rifle. The three of us split up, Johnny coming with
me.

After I wounded the bear, it ran over the crest of the ridge. Following his blood trail, we found him in a wallow under a clump of alder
bushes. He was lying there watching us and at such an angle that I could
not get in a sure head shot. I tried to break his back but the bullet just
missed the spine, although I didn't know it then. It rolled the grizzly half
over. He waved one paw feebly in the air. Then the leg slowly relaxed and
seemed to collapse.

The normal inclination of any hunter would be to run in close enough to
get a head shot if the bruin wasn't quite dead, but I've known enough
grizzlies to have a healthy respect for the clan.

"He's almost done in," Johnny said, "but not quite."

"If I could just see his head," I mused, half to myself.

"You want me to make him lift his head?" the guide asked.

"Don't you go in there," I barked.

Johnny grinned and picked up a small stone.

"I didn't get this old fooling around the head of a live grizzly. This is as
good as any way to make him look up."

We were no more than fifty or sixty feet from the animal. The pebble hit
close to its head. The result was not at all what we expected. One instant the
grizzly lay there, apparently dead, or close to it. The next he was charging
us with a roar that seemed to shake the ground. I had only one shell left in

the chamber and am sure it was instinct that told me to wait until the bear was so close I couldn't miss. I suppose Johnny thought I was terrified into immobility. Anyway he didn't wait to find out. He took off up the mountain side like a jet climbing out of the airport. The grizzly turned from me and went after him, but evidently it was hurting too much to charge far. Just as I was about to pull the trigger, the bear turned and went back to its hollow under the alders. Then it raised its head to look at me, and I shot it between the eyes. Both the guide and I saw it flatten out against the ground.

The immediate sequel to that little scene even more dramatically proved to me that you can't take a "dead" animal for granted. While we had been on the blood trail of the first bear, a second grizzly had raised to its hind legs about three hundred yards down the slope to see what was going on. He was at an angle between the other hunter and me. We both put enough lead into the bear to make him lie down. Later, while Johnnie and I were playing footsie with the first grizzly, we heard my companion shoot several times. When the shooting stopped, we assumed that either the bear or hunter was no longer with us.

"Let's leave this one die good and dead," I suggested to Johnny, "while we go down and skin out the second bear."

We found my companion hunter standing over a bruin now totally deceased, so we skinned it out. While the other hunter and I packed the hide to where we had left the horses at the foot of the ridge, Johnny threw a couple of shells into my rifle and climbed to where we'd left the first bear. We were to bring the horses around while he skinned it out.

Johnny found the grizzly where we'd left it in the alder clump. It looked so dead that he waded in without the usual precautions. Johnny was only a few yards away when the bear stood up and lunged at him. Johnny threw up my rifle, shot the grizzly in the chest, then took off down the mountain with the bear just shirttail distance behind, roaring and swinging at him with every bound. At full speed, Johnny managed to bolt in the second shell and aim the gun back over his shoulder, with the muzzle almost touching the animal. He pulled the trigger, threw down the rifle and ran for his life.

Luckily that last bullet broke the grizzly's back and killed it, but the guide took no more chances. Half an hour later when we brought up the horses, we found him at a safe distance on the hillside, still throwing rocks at the motionless bear.

I never had the privilege of hunting with Johnny Luster again, but I would lay odds that any accident which may have happened to him since our day on the mountain was not caused by a wounded game animal.

BULLET PLACEMENT

From the reaction of any animal when a bullet strikes it, an experienced gunner can usually tell where he scored the hit. If a deer or other hoofed animal humps its back, this is normally the sign of a gut shot, and the best

When hunting trophy-size bear, like the grizzly in these drawings, try to avoid the brain shot. Though lethal, the brain shot can disfigure the mount and split the skull, disqualifying it from official recognition. Then, since a lung-shot bear may live long enough to get into heavy cover or to work you over, aim for the heart or spine.

bet is to get in another hunk of lead as quickly and effectively as possible. A gut-shot bear will often bite at its wound. For a bear, the brain shot is possibly the most lethal, but almost any trophy hunter will avoid this. The skulls of such creatures as bears and mountain lions may be so fragmented by a heavy bullet that they cannot be measured. On antlered game there's a good chance of splitting the skull and causing the antlers to separate at the base so that no matter how large the antlers, they cannot be measured or considered for the record books.

One of the most effective shots is to the upper half of the neck. A solid hit with a high-powered, expanding bullet snaps the neck vertebrae and death is instantaneous. A lower neck shot above the shoulders will put an animal down and keep it there if the bullet strikes the neck vertebrae and spinal cord. A spinal shot farther back is just as lethal. I once killed a bull elk on a mountainside that was so straight up that although I was trying for the lung and heart area, the bullet ranged upward and broke the bull's back.

A dead-center heart shot normally fells an animal on the spot. But you've got to know that the heart is located in the lower part of the chest cavity. If

As with bear, avoid the brain shot on trophy deer because it will disfigure the mount and possibly split the skull, making measurement unreliable. The neck shot can mar the mount too. So aim for the heart-lung area or for the spine.

you have a broadside shot, the spot to place your bullet is immediately behind the lower tip of the shoulder blade. Most riflemen I know try for this general region of the heart and lungs. A bullet through the lungs will kill an animal, but it doesn't always kill quickly. If it knocks the critter down and you are reasonably certain you've made a lung shot, it's not a bad idea to take your time and try to break the neck while the animal lies there.

Almost any gunner with a string of kills behind him has had to track lung-shot game by the blood trail, sometimes for incredible distances. If a lung-shot animal gets away from you, don't rush him. After he thinks he's safely away, he'll lie down in a thicket and watch his back trail. Sit down for half an hour or more before you follow him up and even then go slowly and cautiously. The chances are that you'll find him where he first lay down.

BEING "DEAD" CERTAIN

When you approach your elk, deer, bear or any big-game animal, the most important fact you want to establish is that it's dead. Take your time. Keep your gun loaded and ready. Don't get too close until you are sure that your "kill" won't jump to its feet and disappear into the brush, or charge and hurt you.

Certain indications will tell you whether your game is still alive. The two most obvious are movement and breathing. These do not necessarily mean that the creature is not fatally wounded or that it will not die on the spot. If the downed animal is laboring to stay alive, the humane thing to do is shoot it again in the neck. Or if you know it has no trophy possibilities, shoot it in the head.

Almost any old timer will tell you that if an animal's eyes are closed, no matter how lifeless it may otherwise seem, don't take a chance. A creature normally dies with its eyes open, and in just a little while the eyes begin to glaze over. But if the animal is lying there in a comfortable position, possibly with the head stretched out, its eyes closed and its ears either laid back or erect, the odds are very good that it's not dead and could be waiting for you to get close enough.

The position of a "kill" often indicates whether the animal is dead. If it is sprawled out at a grotesque angle or in an unnatural position, with ears flopped and tongue out, you can normally be sure of no more activity. But even then, follow through to the last precaution. Throw rocks or sticks from a safe position. Hit the head if possible. Work your way close enough to touch the pupil of the eye with a long stick. This is one of the most sensitive parts. If the eye doesn't blink or show some reaction, you may be reasonably sure that all of its life has gone. While you're doing all this, keep you gun ready. And *never* get too close until you are "dead" certain.

Around every hunting camp, someone always comes up with a story of an excited or careless hunter who went to his game too quickly after it had been shot down. It's only natural that a few of the stories are intended to raise the stature of the teller—hunters being what they are. But there is enough evidence of what a wounded animal can do to a man to make one believe many of these accounts. Buck deer have gotten up and run off after they were tagged, to be bagged later by another hunter in the vicinity. And similar incidents have been verified throughout the country.

This has never happened to anyone I know, but several times I've heard of the fellow who lodges his rifle in the antlers of a fallen big buck before stepping back to take a picture. With the cameraman poised, the deer suddenly gets up and is gone with the rifle on its rack. The hunter usually recovers his gun, along the buck's line of flight, with a broken scope or stock.

A friend and fellow writer, George Laycock, who wrote one of the top books on deer hunting, told me about one of his outdoor partners who threw a small buck he'd just downed, into the trunk of his car with the intention of field dressing it at home, just a few miles away. When the fellow raised the trunk lid in his back yard, the buck, only stunned by the shot, jumped out and disappeared into the nearby woods.

But the hunter who loses a buck upon opening the car trunk and the fellow who has his rifle carried off on the buck's antlers are comparatively lucky. Every year several hunters in this country are hurt and occasionally some are killed by going too quickly to the fallen game and laying a hand on it. We are not as likely to hear of such foolishness with bears and some of the other big-game animals which are usually approached with caution. But since the deer is a smaller and more innocent-looking animal, stories are rather common of guys who lay aside the gun before grabbing a buck by its hind leg. When these guys pull the buck over and start the gutting operation, they suddenly find themselves kicked into the middle of next week because of the animal's reaction. That sharp hoof on a powerful hind leg can break bones and leave a serious wound.

Rather general, too, are the accounts of the man who bends over the front end of a deer to stick or cut its throat to bleed it, only to discover that his trophy did not take at all well to the idea of being bled. Some of these fellows have been hurt, and seriously.

The most bizarre of the risen-from-the-dead tales I've heard was sworn to me by a couple of outdoor partners whose word I have no reason to doubt. One of them shot down a fair buck and went immediately to it. The other, on a nearby stand, heard the shot and came up just in time to see his companion lean his gun against a tree trunk before straddling the deer to pull its head up and cut its throat. About that time the buck recovered from its superficial wound. Leaping straight up with the hunter on its back and holding onto its antlers, the buck took off through the thicket. The would-be deer slayer lost his knife and his hat. In the hundred feet he rode the terrified deer, he lost so much of his hunting jacket and pants that they wouldn't have made a suitable gift to a beggar. The hunter wasn't badly hurt, but he was somewhat shaken up, scratched, bruised and disenchanted with bronco buck riding.

So when you approach your animal, don't be at all reluctant to shoot again if there's any doubt about life in your trophy. One of the other critters that reinforced this lesson was a buck antelope in Wyoming.

I thought I had shot down enough game to have a pretty good idea as to when an animal was fatally wounded. I found that I didn't know as much as I thought, and it cost me a much better than average antelope head.

When Bill Rae was editor of *Outdoor Life* and I was one of the field editors, we made a good many trips together, hither and yon throughout these United States, to catch up with such creatures as deer, elk, wild turkeys and other game, as well as most of the kinds of fish. We went to Wyoming sev-

Having learned the hard way on other hunts, the author here made certain this bull was dead before approaching for the cameraman.

eral times after the hooved critters, and some of our most interesting days were on the great plains of that state. We took pronghorns in a number of regions scattered from Cheyenne to Cody, but no hunt was more intriguing than that around Lost Cabin, about 70 miles northwest of Casper.

For two days we were after a long-horned buck with a good spread. By that time I was becoming thoroughly convinced that the animal knew more about hunting than we did. He certainly was familiar with the lay of the land. He always traveled, grazed or lay down where not even a jack rabbit could approach within a mile without being seen.

One day as we watched the buck from about two miles away, he lay down for his noonday siesta. We were on the crest of a low rolling ridge that overlooked a big basin, which appeared as flat as the inside of a frying pan. The only break I could see was a shallow wash that ran at an angle off the ridge. By staying low enough in the wash, I though I might at least reach the flat where the antelope was — without being seen.

"I'm going after him," I announced.

"If you get closer than half a mile," my partner chuckled, "I'll treat you to a Coke."

I made the base of the slope all right, except that my knees were all out of shape from having to stay below the gully rim. I was pleased to see that the flat, which had appeared so unbroken from the ridge, was veined with small arroyos. One of these put me within four-hundred yards of the animal on his downwind side. When I peeped over the edge of the arroyo, all I could see were the tips of the animal's horns. Collecting sand in my shirt and prickly pear needles in my hide as I went, I crawled more than three-hundred yards to a slight break in the flat. Bill told me later that I was on this tortuous journey more than an hour and a half. When I couldn't go any closer without being seen, I very carefully propped myself up behind a clump of sagebrush and sat there until I was composed and breathing normally. All I could see from that position was the pronghorn's head and top of his back. He was angled in such a way that I decided to try for a back-bone shot that would break his back or penetrate down into the lung and heart cavity.

When I pulled the trigger, the antelope rolled over and lay still. I jumped up and ran toward him, my gun ready. I put my sights on him when he staggered to his feet, weaved back and forth, and then toppled over. I was so sure that this was his dying gasp that I slung the gun over my shoulder and walked toward my trophy. I got within several yards of him before he was suddenly on his feet, running as only an antelope can run. Before I could get the gun off my shoulder and into my hands, the animal had disappeared into a little draw. When he came in sight again, he was three-hundred yards away and making tracks. I shot at him three times and missed.

We hunted that pronghorn for the remainder of the day, saw him at a distance several times, but never got close enough for another blow. All afternoon I berated myself because I had not put in the clincher bullet, and could only hope that the first one had not hurt him too badly and that he would survive. After making all that stalk, I simply had not read the signs right. Nor have I ever failed since to put in that second bullet if there were even a question of whether one was needed.

HOW TO GET "TORE UP"

Only once have I ever deliberately crawled up to an animal I knew was alive. In this case, except for the interference of a benign providence that forgave my stupidity and a herculean guide with a razor-sharp machete, it would have been my last crawl.

We were hunting wild boars in the jungles of the West Indies. Our dogs had run a tremendous brute of a boar for an hour or more and finally bayed it in a dense thicket. I had run and fallen over the rocky, moss-covered ground until I was near exhaustion. By the time the guide and I reached the thicket, I was pretty much done in. The boar had backed up against a low, limestone ledge with three dogs in front of him. All I wanted was to photograph the dramatic scene. Unarmed, I crawled into that thicket with my camera. The pig's attention was on the dogs. And maybe he thought I was just part of the pack until my flash bulb went off. Then he broke through the circle of dogs and charged me.

Fortunately the guide happened to be in the right place and knew what to do. I wasn't wasting time or sparing shrubbery getting out of there but wouldn't have made it on my own. The man with the machete leaped in between us. His blow was so powerful that it slashed through the brush and knocked the big boar off its feet. The guide fell on top of the pig to hold it down and since there was no room and he was in no position to swing his machete, he dropped it and seized a heavy knot of wood lying near. With the boar's heavy tusks slashing back and forth within inches of his face, the guide beat the animal into submission and tied first its feet and then its snout with heavy cord. Those few minutes of battle were the most brutal and fierce I have ever seen between two creatures.

LUNG SHOTS

Depending on how the bullet strikes it, a lung-shot animal dies quickly or is capable of going a long distance before it succumbs. The lungs may quickly or slowly fill with blood, which ultimately suffocates the animal. But if you are close enough to listen and have heard the sounds before, you will know when the animal dies.

We hunted two weeks in Alaska's vast delta country west of Anchorage, in the big flat region near the mouth of the Kuskokwim River. During that time we might have seen the sun, but I doubt it. All I remember is rain. The country was loaded with big brown bears that congregated to feed on the salmon that collected to spawn in the heads of the creeks. I spent a good bit of time on a little hillside overlooking a marsh. Broad game trails ran along the winding creeks and shallow pools below where we sat waiting for a glimpse of an outsized brownie. The continuous rain and high humidity kept my scope fogged and finally clouded it over, inside and outside.

Not being enough of a gun expert to know about such things, I unscrewed as many of the lenses as possible and wiped them free of fog. In so doing, I removed the scope's spider thread crosshairs.

Shortly after this happened, the big brownie we'd been waiting for came down a creekside trail and waded into one of the shallow pools for a salmon. I looked at him a couple of hundred yards away through the scope, which was now only a 4-power glass.

My guide was a nice, pleasant fellow who had come to Alaska only recently as a tractor operator and somehow had wangled himself a guide's license. He wasn't the best woodsman I ever knew and I'd brought him back to camp a couple of times when he got turned around. I had no idea how reliable he would be when the chips were really down. I can only guess that a streak of recklessness popped up in me.

"He's too far without the crosshairs," I whispered. "Let's get closer."

The marsh grass was about shoulder high. The wind was in our favor. And we had no trouble approaching within fifty yards of the brownie. I thought that was close enough. The guide had already begun to lag some yards to the rear, which probably proved that he was more sensible than I.

I put the bear's lung area as near as I could get it in the center of the scope. The 220-grain chunk of lead knocked him on his side in the shallow pond. He recovered quickly and scrambled up the far bank that lifted to a small wooded knoll on the edge of the marsh. My second bullet, which I'm sure was tagged with luck, knocked him down again. I was just as pleased when he went out of sight over a little hillock. The guide and I walked to the upper edge of the pond and listened. We heard a bit of thrashing, then the coarse, raspy breathing that indicated a lung shot. By now the guide had recovered some of his bravado.

"He's had it! Let's go get him!"

He lifted his foot to step into the shallow pool.

"You go," I said. "I'll wait here until I hear him die."

He withdrew his foot to its original position, and we stood there listening to the breaths which grew more labored. I stifled the inclination to go ahead anyway and put the bear out of its pain. I believe that I actually suffered those few minutes with him and was relieved when the last shuddering gasps told me that it was all over.

I knew the brownie was dead but still didn't take a chance or let the guide take one. Holding a gun ready, we threw sticks from a safe distance and even after there was no reaction, approached cautiously. After I touched the eye pupil with a very long stick and nothing moved, I continued to wait a minute or two to be sure our potential rug was not playing possum.

It's not pleasant to hear a lung-shot animal die. I much prefer a clean, sudden kill. Whenever possible, I put a dying creature to sleep as quickly as I can. In this instance it might have been possible but decidedly risky.

BOTH SIDES OF DRINK

This chapter, which deals to a large extent with carelessness, is as good a point as any to put in a word about alcohol and hunting. A guy, hopped up with the false courage a drink can give him, may take chances far beyond anything he would do while cold-thinking sober.

I'm not against alcohol in its proper place and in the proper amounts. I am against its use by anyone while engaged in any outdoor pursuit, especially hunting and fishing. No matter how well he can hold his liquor, a man in a boat is more likely to have some degree of bad judgment with even one drink in him and make a move which will endanger his own life and the lives of others.

The same holds true of the gunner. Alcohol in the blood begins to swell and block out those brain cells in the frontal or "judgment" lobe of the brain. As far as I know, no one has ever tabulated the extent to which drink has been the cause of "accidental" deaths by a hunter's bullet or of injuries caused when a shooter dashes up to the game he has downed, without taking the proper precautions.

One humorous story concerning hunting and drink was told to me by Floy Scroggins, who conducts an outdoor radio show and issues a weekly news bulletin on her favorite Beaver Lake in northwest Arkansas.

Floy's story concerns two deer hunters in the Arkansas mountains who left their truck and went in opposite directions to hunt. They stayed at it most of the day.

One finally got a good buck. He was dragging it back to the truck and had paused to rest when another whitetail with a huge rack walked out and stood within range. The hunter had not heard his buddy shoot, so figured he would help by collecting his partner's trophy for him.

You guessed it! His companion was already at the truck with a buck and rack of his own.

Instead of leaving one deer to spoil, they decided to be honest about it, look up the nearest game warden, report the error and take the consequences.

On the way they passed another pickup truck with a hunter in it, asleep. They tried to wake him, but couldn't. Further investigation indicated that apparently he had taken a few nips too many.

So they put one of the bucks in the back of his pickup and took the live shell out of his rifle, replacing it with an empty hull one of them had saved for reloading and which was the same caliber as that of the drunk's gun. They drove off without disturbing him.

3

Field-dressing Hoofed Game

When We Were somewhere high in the Wyoming Rockies and had just downed our buck or bull with "one well-placed shot"—though the well-placed was not always the first one—I've heard my old mountain friend and guide Max Wilde say literally dozens of times, "Well, when you kill, the fun of hunting is over."

Overall, that is not quite true. The "fun" of big game hunting includes a great many pleasures of which the gun is only a small part. High mountain trails when you are in the saddle, wind in the spruce forests, sudden storms, pitching a tent in a lofty alpine meadow, rugged canyons, the world above timberline—these remain in memory after you've bagged your trophy. *I have always maintained that pulling the trigger is the poorest part of any big-game hunt.*

In a more literal sense, perhaps, Max was right. The excitement of spotting the animal, the stalk and getting into position, and barreling in that well-placed bullet come to a halt when your game is on the ground. Now you have to go to work. What you do in the next thirty minutes and in the next thirty hours, will more than often dictate the quality of your meat and what kind of trophy the taxidermist will enable you to hang on your den wall.

Wild meat is considered by those who know how to handle it properly as among nature's most delicious comestibles, though there are many persons who claim that they cannot tolerate the "wild" flavor. We once had a city friend who said that the meat of any wild animal nauseated him, and I supposed it did mainly because he knew what he was eating. We invited him over to a steak dinner and I char-broiled elk T-bones exactly the way I would have cooked the steaks off a steer. The elk meat had been properly aged and cut and was "prime" by domestic standards. My friend declared it was the best steak he had ever tasted. We never did tell him the difference.

Generally a person doesn't like wild meat because he has tasted some which was not properly handled and treated. It always saddens me to see some young fellow who has killed his first whitetail buck, probably with a rib or belly shot that made a mess of the insides, plus maybe another slug in the hindquarters, drag his deer out of the woods without field-dressing it, throw it over the hot hood of his automobile and drive it around town for half a day showing it off to friends. I know what kind of eating he'll get out of that when he finally delivers it to some butcher to be processed, or tries to do the job himself.

Not quite as bad is the fellow who does gut his deer immediately, then brings it to his home, hangs it up to finish the skinning and butchering, and puts his meat into the deep freezer before it's hardly cold. If you want to make wild meat tender and tasty, you must put it through an aging process —the kind pen-raised beef receives. The fattest corn-fed Angus steer would be less than palatable if it were shot down on a sandy or dirty hillside, with several chunks of lead in its belly and other places, left there for a few hours before gutting, dragged around in the dirt, then skinned out, chopped into manageable portions and crammed into the freezer—all in short order.

With wild meat the best favor you can do for yourself is to field-dress it as quickly as possible. Wild meat spoils if left for even a short time. A few years ago in Wyoming's Thorofare, one of our hunters rode on ahead of the party, took a wrong trail and got lost. Late in the afternoon he came on a big bull elk feeding in one of the parks bordering the trail. He got off his horse, jacked a shell into the chamber and felled the elk where it stood. Believing that the guides were immediately behind him and would dress out the bull when they found it, the fellow tied his red bandana on a stick and arranged it over the animal so that it would attract attention from the trail. Then he rode on until dark, whereupon he realized that he was lost and stopped for the night.

At daylight the next morning we picked up the lost man's trail. Half an hour later we found the dead bull. Although the night had been close to freezing and no sunshine had touched the animal, it was as bloated as if it had been there a week, and of course the meat was spoiled. It saddened me that this magnificent animal would go to waste for the lack of less than half an hour needed to open it and pull out the insides.

KNIVES

To do this job our wanderer would have needed no more than his pocket knife. Most hunters, however, carry sheath knives on their belts and some haul along additional tools, such as a small belt ax. I have generally found that the more experience a man has had with dressing animals, the shorter his knife will be.

I grew up in an era of outsized belt knives. If I didn't have at least a nine-inch blade, it wasn't "fitten" to whittle a toothpick. A "genuine" Bowie knife was the dream of every lad who figured he was big enough to take to the woods. You could do everything with it from chopping logs for a campfire, to sticking wild redskins—if there had been any wild redskins. As for peeling a deer, the big knife was a mite long and awkward.

Long ago I concluded that the kind and size of knife a man carries in the woods, depends on what he thinks he'll need it for. Knives range from a two-foot machete for hacking out a trail to the small folding pocket variety. Once in Mississippi when I left my sheath knife in camp, I field-dressed two bucks with a two-inch blade in the pocket knife given to me by Bo Randall, the famous knife maker. No more than three inches in length, ³/₄-inch wide and ¼-inch thick, that knife carries two blades and four tools I have found useful.

Most top outdoorsmen I know are very set in their opinions about knives. Some do not favor any of the belt varieties on the basis that they are in the way, or catch on brush which often pulls them out of their sheath. The best type of scabbard to correct this is the one that covers both the blade and handle of the knife and leaves no part to catch on limbs, brush or clothing. A large percentage of those who wear belt knives prefer one with a four- or five-inch thin blade. My own choice is the five-inch but I have no special reason other than habit over many years.

On a big-game hunt, I often carry a folding knife with a five-inch blade that locks in place. On the opposite end is a five-inch saw blade that also folds into the knife. I've used this saw innumerable times for cutting through the pelvic bone and brisket where in a large game animal they were too tough to cut through with the knife blade. Many guides carry a small hatchet in their saddle bags for this purpose. A few hunters I know pack along a Gerber steel, which is a kind of wide, heavy chisel that can be pounded through the bone with a rock or heavy stick. Using this steel is much better than trying to pound your hunting knife blade through by hammering on the back of it. I've seen some mighty good knives mutilated in this manner, usually by neophytes.

One important item to have in your pocket or pack is a good whetstone or sharpening steel. The tough hide of an animal and the bones with which the knife comes in contact can dull the finest blade. I carry both steel and stone, the steel being no more than six inches long and ¼-inch in diameter, and the stone about one by three inches. The steel does a quick rough job and the stone quickly smooths it up.

THE CASE OF THE PURLOINED MEAT

Occasionally guides—but almost no hunters—carry much more elaborate equipment for dressing out an animal. When I downed a caribou or moose, guides have drawn out a small meat saw to help put English on a dressing-out job. Out of at least a couple of freight-car loads of elk, the very best meat bull I almost had was one that Dick Loftsgarten and I put on the ground above Buffalo Bill's famous T E Ranch in northwest Wyoming. Dick and I were specifically after meat and when we spotted a small, fat four-pointer lying in a little draw, I left my partner with the horses and worked my way by foot to a place uphill from the bull. I shot down through the back of the neck. The bull didn't move six inches from where it lay. We gutted it out, and I proposed quartering it and hauling the carcass to the ranch on my saddle horse.

"It's better to let it cool out overnight," Dick suggested. "We'll bring a meat saw back tomorrow and do a bang-up job."

The next morning we carried a pack horse with us. I watched my saddle partner operate on that elk with the skill of a professional butcher. There wasn't a mark on it except at the place where I'd broken its neck.

At the ranch we hung the meat in his dry cooling room and left it there for a month. I'd gone back to my home in Georgia long before that. So to save Dick Loftsgarten a lot of trouble, I called one of my old guides in Cody and asked him to pick up my meat, have it processed at the locker plant, and ship it to me collect.

When the box of frozen meat arrived at my house, I opened it up, my mouth watering with the thought of all those elk steaks, chops and roasts which had been given the proper treatment to make it A-1, first class, prime meat. What I found in the bottom of that box was two-hundred pounds of elk bologna, which you make out of meat too tough to do anything with but put through the grinder and stuff into sausage skins.

When I called my old friend (friend?) and guide in Cody to ask what happened to the meat I'd left at Dick Loftsgarten's, he said, "I understand that was the way you wanted it fixed."

I'm a long way from being a Sherlock Holmes and I didn't accuse the old friend. But as plain as the nose on my face was the fact that he'd hung my good meat in his freezer-locker and dug out the bologna that possibly was made from a trophy bull so old and tough that the dude who shot it just gave it to the guide. There wasn't much the guide could do with the meat except grind it up—and send it to me!

That winter the guide who had pulled that stunt took a trip to visit some of his clients scattered around the states, and I was one of them. He stayed for a week in our home. I suppose he would have stayed longer had we not been most careful to see that he ate that elk bologna every day for breakfast, lunch and dinner. I think he finally got the message and also began to suspect that I wasn't entirely duped by his maneuver. For the next year he offered me a free hunt with all the trimmings in one of his best elk territories.

HOW TO FIELD-DRESS

Of course you can't always have a real pro like Dick Loftsgarten along to dress game out every time you score. Nor do you always have a guide along who knows his business. You may be able to turn the meat over to a local butcher for skinning and cutting, but generally that field-dressing job is up to you. And the quality of meat largely depends on the field-dressing.

The method of field-dressing an animal hangs on a number of conditions—among them are the size of the kill, the terrain, and the hunter's experience or lack of it.

There are conflicting views on what should and should not be done after a hunter approaches his game and determines that it is dead. If he is a tyro and has heard that all meat should be bled to make it palatable, his first move will either be to cut the animal's throat and thereby ruin a good cape if it's a trophy, or he'll stick his hunting knife into the base of the throat, feeling for one of the main arteries off the heart.

Maybe my acquaintance is not as wide as it should be, but most of the old-time guides I know tell me that this bleeding is totally unnecessary, and often results in mutilation of hide and meat. One pointed out that in the first place, when the heart has stopped, it no longer pumps blood from the arteries and veins. Although the arteries and veins will drain, the process is slow. A certain percentage of the blood is found in the body cavity and can be eliminated if the carcass is field-dressed immediately. At least some of the remaining blood will drain out of the warm body if it is laid out or hung in the proper position.

On the other hand, my favorite butcher, Emory Willis, has more savvy about pen-raised or wild meat than any man I know. He claims that where no trophy is involved, cutting the large artery in the throat of a deer, immediately after it is killed, and dragging the head into a downhill position so that the deer will drain better, makes for a better piece of meat. The reason venison is usually dark, Willis says, is that the network of small veins is still filled with blood. A bullet that cuts blood vessels in the heart or other front part of the body cavity will cause blood to collect in the cavity.

Some experts vow that the tarsal and metatarsal glands of hoofed animals should be cut off immediately and that the genitals should be removed so that they will not affect the flavor of the meat. Others claim this is pure rubbish—that if these parts do not taint the meat while the animal is alive, the only way they taint it after he's dead is by being transferred to the meat from the knife blade. I've watched my guides skin out dozens of elk, sheep, caribou and others and have never yet seen a guide bother with the scent glands. I've seen a few guides remove the genitals before they start gutting, but the consensus is that they can be taken off any time, since they do not affect the meat in one way or another.

There are even two schools of thought on whether an animal should be gutted from back to front, or whether you should start at the top of the stomach and go to the tail. I don't believe that either would have any great advantage over the other, but most of the animals I have dressed or seen dressed were started at the anus.

Should the kill be hung up, partially hung up or left on the ground for field dressing? There are guys who swear by each position, but the simplest and easiest way to handle the cavity contents seems to be with the creature on its back, the upper part of its body slightly uphill.

There are also different ideas about cleaning the body cavity of blood and other matter not pulled out with the main contents. Hunters have told me that they wash the cavity with water where water is available. One of my acquaintances says he carries along a box of salt and mixes salt water to wash out the body after the insides are removed. Then he wipes it dry. I asked Emory Willis about this and he says that water, fresh or salt, doesn't hurt the meat.

"We never process a deer without first washing it out inside," he declares. "It helps if the hunter washes out the cavity when he field-dresses his buck or doe, especially if there is bloodshot meat there. We've even saved some bloody meat by giving it several soakings in cold water."

Emory' reference to bleeding and washing concerned the whitetail deer in middle Georgia. But I'm sure he would get a lot of argument from many northern and most western guides, especially where elk, moose, caribou and other large game are involved. I was raised in the dry school, possibly because most of the time no rinse water was available, and had it been, we couldn't have hauled enough in our bandanas or hands to do the job.

Whether or not you wash out a carcass, a good rule of thumb is to drain or dry it by wiping the cavity as clean as possible.

And whether you decide to hang, bleed, wash, remove scent glands or whatever, you should follow a number of basic steps in field-dressing your big game.

Unless the temperature is so far below zero that you are likely to quick-freeze, take off your coat and roll up your sleeves. Even when you go about it right, gutting a creature is normally a messy, bloody job. And before you know it, you'll have gore half way to your elbows. Disposable plastic gloves help for this job. I've been with a couple of fellows who put them on, causing raised eyebrows among the old-timers standing around. But you don't really need the gloves. Blood washes off easily.

One of your first steps is getting the animal into position for gutting. Having the head uphill makes this chore easier, both for making the necessary cuts and rolling out the cavity contents after they have been cut loose. If the slope is too steep the animal will slide as you work with it. Several times I've found it necessary to tie the head to a tree so that I could turn and twist the body, and not have it slide or roll over me.

To raise an animal for the gutting process, some fellows suggest the following procedure: Bend a sapling over, tying the head to it. Then make a tripod hoist by cutting two or three forked poles and placing them in a tepee arrangement. This allows you to raise the animal by moving one pole in at a time.

Another simple method of raising a heavy animal requires a stout fourteen- or fifteen-foot pole employed as a lever. You need three ropes, one at each end and one about two or three feet from the short, heavy end. You use

HANGING HEAVY GAME

By moving one pole in at a time, you can raise heavy game with this tripod.

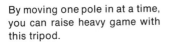

With the leverage that a pole and three lengths of rope provide, you can raise game twice your weight.

the rope at the fulcrum point to suspend your pole from a heavy tree limb. This accomplished, secure the rope on the short end of the pole to the head or base of the antlers. By pulling down on the long end of the pole, you can lift and hold up the head or front end of an animal.

Whether on the ground or suspended, the animal should be positioned to make the job of gutting easy for you.

As we pointed out, some dressers start at one end and some at the other. All the guides I know first flesh out the genitals. This you can accomplish by grasping them in one hand and cutting the skin all around without cutting the organs themselves or the intestinal wall. Then lay the penis back and cut it free from the pelvic arch.

Next continue the cut around the vent just at the base of the tail. The vent is surrounded by a tough, pliable tissue, best attacked with a sharp knife. Cut *around* the vent without puncturing it. Few of the wilderness big game guides I know ever bother to do this, but many hunters cut the vent loose on all sides until it may be pulled out far enough to be tied with a short string to keep the excretion inside. I carry string in my shoulder bag or hunting coat pocket for many purposes, and this is one of them. A rubber band wound tightly around the intestine outlet is just as good.

Turn the animal on its back or as close to this position as possible. How easy this is depends on the animal's size. If it's a moose or elk, or other very large animal, you may need help. This is one of the many reasons for having along a guide or hunting partner. You can man-handle a small hoofed animal and hold it in place by propping one of its hind legs behind your knee. With a larger animal, it may be necessary to lift the front portion partially off the ground using the tepee or pole arrangement. One of my hunting partners carries a light-weight block and tackle in his pack.

After cutting around the genitals and vent, put two fingers under the skin and muscle of the lower abdomen and lift it away from the intestines. The cavity contents will press against the back of your hand, so push down and hold them away from the knife blade as it cuts up the center of the belly, along the line held by your two fingers. Make this cut all the way to the top of the body cavity or to that line at the top of the belly where you will cut to take off the cape for your trophy mount. Caping will be explained in Chapter 6.

If the head of your animal is uphill, gravity will pull the insides toward you. Now you will notice the diaphragm, a strong layer of muscular tissue that separates the chest cavity from the abdominal cavity and holds the organs in place.

Now you get into the dirty part of your job, especially if the bullet has passed through the guts or the rib cage. Reach up into the cavity with your knife and, with the other hand pressing down the organs, cut the diaphragm loose from the rib cage—starting at the top, with sweeping strokes down both sides. With your other hand, you can feel the body contents give and come loose. Then you can turn the animal on its side and roll the body

STEPS FOR FIELD-DRESSING

For a more detailed description also see the author's text.

Flesh out the genitals and cut around the vent without cutting into the organs themselves or the intestinal wall.

Work two fingers under the skin and muscle of the lower abdomen and lift this away from the intestines while cutting up toward the breastbone.

Pressing on the visceral contents, cut the diaphragm loose from the rib cage.

Then turn the animal on its side and roll the contents onto the ground. A few knife strokes around the vent should completely free the insides and allow you to pull them out. Now you can rescue edible parts such as the heart and liver.

After sawing through the pelvic bone, saw through the breastbone and remove as much of the windpipe as possible. The windpipe would otherwise spoil.

contents out on the ground. The next few strokes of your knife around the vent should completely free the insides so that you can pull them out by hand.

Some hunters go about it differently, but my next move is to cut through the pelvic bone so that I can spread the hind legs, which further opens the body cavity and gives me more room to complete the field-dressing.

I've operated on small deer with pelvic bones soft enough to cut through with a knife. Normally, however, a small hatchet comes in handy at this point, or I use the saw blade on that big folding knife I carry. I shudder when a guy batters up a good hunting knife by beating it through the pelvic bone with a rock.

Since it doesn't take long, my next step is to rescue the edible parts from the insides. My choices are the liver and the heart; they are delectable portions of all hoofed game. I take out the liver and remove the gall sac. I operate carefully but even if I make a mistake and slice into the gall, the meat will not absorb the gall, which can be washed off. I cut the heart loose, peel the pericardium (membrane sac) from around it and drop the liver and heart into a plastic bag. When water is available, I pour some in the bottom of my plastic bag to keep the liver and heart from drying out too quickly.

I am fond of liver, but one of my choices of all wild meats is elk heart. Boiled, it has been the basis for many a noonday sandwich, munched while I sat on a mountainside and gloried in the magnificent scenery laid out before me.

A hoofed animal carries many other edible parts. The exact number depends on just how far you want to go. Some hunters like the tongue, and it's a good piece of meat. Others have a tooth for the kidneys. When I mention that kidneys might carry a scent from the bladder, these hunters assure me that water washes the scent away.

One of the food items overlooked is the brain of a hoofed animal. Several times I've been with guides who know how delectable "brains" are and go to some pains to save them when sawing off the top of the skull with attached antlers. My wife buys pig brains and calf brains in the market and scrambles them with eggs. But they can't compare with the cranium contents of a moose, caribou, elk or deer.

Some primitive tribes eat every part of a game animal but the squeal, snort, hoofs and hide. They consider boiled eyes a delicacy and they boil the intestinal walls (chitterlings) and even cook and eat what is inside the intestines. Unborn young is a rare treat for them, and they save as much of the blood as they can for the pot. If we were not well fed enough to have become squeamishly civilized, we'd probably do the same. Starving people have fewer qualms about food.

The heart and liver rescued and stowed, let's get back to the carcass. There is much else to do. If I plan to save the cape, I make that cut next, from the lower part of the brisket around the shoulder. Then I peel this back as closely as possible to the base of the antlers or horns. This is discussed in detail in Chapter 6.

If I don't want the cape, I slit the skin to the throat. In either case, I saw lengthwise through the brisket, then reach into the throat and cut off as much of the windpipe as I can. This is one part of an animal that quickly spoils.

I have always made a practice of cutting away and disposing of any bloodshot meat in sight. But my butcher friend tells me that if a hunter can get this to him quickly enough for washing, he can save it without any loss of flavor. This, of course, may not work when you are ten days deep in the wilderness.

One of the objectives of field-dressing any animal as quickly as possible is to reduce body heat, as well as to drain away blood, both of which are spoil factors. After you have removed all inside organs, you should follow one of two or three procedures. If the animal is small enough to be handled, turn it over on its belly with all four legs outstretched. This will help drain out the remaining blood as well as cool the carcass and partially protect it from small meat-eating birds and mammals. If possible, spread the body on needles, leaves, moss or rocks. Avoid sand or dirt, which are difficult to remove from the meat later.

A larger animal, waiting to be quartered and too heavy to arrange belly down, can be propped open with sticks to hasten the cooling. But better methods, those that require more time and effort, are to hang or partially hang the carcass, as shown earlier in this chapter. This allows better drainage and under some conditions will help speed cooling.

4

Field Care, Transport, Skinning, Tanning

You Have Made a successful stalk and a great shot, both of which will improve with each telling and in time become rare vintage. You have gone through the ritual of tagging your game according to the requirements of the state in which you are hunting. The number of pictures you made of the trophy depends on how much of a camera nut you are, or what you think the editors will want if you are a writer. You have gone through the processes of field-dressing your animal to bleed and cool the carcass. You may have caped the animal. (This is covered in Chapter 6.) Your next task is to get your meat and trophy out of the woods.

Most states have laws making it a violation to leave or abandon the meat of any game animal you've killed. I've downed bucks and bulls in such rugged and isolated regions that the question was whether to try to get it out or to set up camp and stay there until we had disposed of the carcass by eating it on the spot. We were never really serious about this, but it did make a lot of good conversation.

How easy or how difficult the salvage of your meat will be depends on many such factors. These include your distance into back country, the size of the animal, the availability of transportation, the weather, and whether you are with a partner or alone.

A sad indication of the present times is the fact that in many regions where hunters are numerous, one doesn't dare leave his trophy or meat for even a little while without fear of having it stolen by another hunter. Each such section of the country has its own stories of the fellow who went back for his four-wheel drive or for help from his buddies to find his kill gone when he returned.

One story going the rounds is about the guy who took an especially good buck. Another hunter came along just as he was dressing it out. The second hunter agreed to stay and guard the deer while the successful nimrod went for his truck. You guessed it again. When the fellow got back with his vehicle, both the deer and its protector were gone.

From what I hear, this is not an isolated case of theft, but it usually occurs in regions where the woods is full of hunters. We would assume that the vast percentage of gunners are honest sportsmen. The sprinkling of scoundrels is to be expected, as it is in any society. In expansive big-game country where hunters are few and scattered, cases of theft are rare if they occur at all.

I try to avoid those areas which contain more gunners than game, but for one reason or another have been in such spots several times in the past few years. A season or two ago I went into the woods by flashlight before daybreak and sat down where I could watch a game trail crossing. One wild pathway came up a shallow valley and another, off a flat ridge, crossed a little creek and climbed the ridge beyond. This was a perfect spot because in the first hour or so of daylight a couple of small deer and half-dozen deer slayers came by. None ever saw me. The hunter-hikers had the deer moving, and when the sun was an hour high I downed a creditable buck.

I field-dressed the buck quickly, then found myself in a dilemma. The buck was too heavy for my aging muscles to shoulder pack or drag uphill the mile or more to my car. I decided to take advantage of an old road that ran within a couple of hundred yards. Fifty yards away was a thicket. Out of this I cut enough tops and boughs to make a blind around my deer and pile of entrails. When I covered them with leaves, they were so well hidden that I wondered if I would be able to find them again. Certainly none but the keenest-eyed woodsman would have noticed my tracks, and I wasn't worried about the honesty of a guy like that.

When I drove the car close and got back to the spot, I saw a hunter coming up the valley. We met within a dozen feet of where my deer lay hidden. We talked for twenty minutes, and he never suspected I'd made a kill. When he strolled on, I dragged the buck to my car.

In big wilderness country I've taken innumerable big-game animals that we gutted and left until we could return the next day with horses to pack them out. There we never feared that the meat would be molested by man. In wolf or coyote country there's a remote possibility that your carcass may be chewed on a bit, but normally these cagey animals suspect a trap of some kind and avoid fresh-killed meat with the scent of man around it. Bears have never bothered a carcass we left overnight except once in Alaska, when we downed a bull caribou on a mountain about an hour's ride from camp. We had no pack horse with us. And since it was late afternoon, we dressed-out and caped the bull and then left the carcass to pick up the next day.

When we arrived again at the kill site, the caribou was gone. About the only indications that it had ever been there were some blood on the ground and several Canada jays picking at scraps of offal. We figured the dressed carcass had weighed between 200 and 250 pounds. Overnight, it had vanished as completely as if it had been lifted off the ridge with a helicopter.

Our Indian guide was a good tracker. He began to circle for sign and some minutes later called to us from down the slope. In a soft spot he'd found the track of an enormous grizzly. Then he found another farther down the slope, but there was no place we could see where the carcass had been dragged. Beyond that the tracks disappeared in the moss and on the rocky ground.

There was no other sign except in a couple of places, but the heavy prints deep in the soft earth indicated that the bear might have been carrying a load. We took a line on the general direction he traveled and spread out to cover as much of the semi-barren slope as possible.

We found the caribou — or what was left of it — partially hidden in a dry wash about 600 yards from where we'd last seen it. Apparently the bear had picked that heavy carcass up in his jaws, gone downhill through a little creek valley then up the side of the mountain for at least a hundred yards. If the caribou had touched or dragged anywhere, we could not find the spot.

What an enormous brute the bear must have been! Hoping he might have fed and moved off a little way to sleep off his feast, we searched around in the likely spots. But for some reason the bear had moved on, so we didn't get a shot.

FIELD CARE OF MEAT

The immediate treatment of your freshly killed meat depends on a number of things, such as the weather, the size of the animal and the length of time you plan to leave the meat before getting it to your home or camp.

When the weather is warm, as it is in many of the southern, early deer seasons, clouds of flies seem to materialize out of nowhere. They range from a dull color to bright metallic blue or green. They lay their eggs in the meat, upon which the larvae will feed when hatched. In some warm weather areas, the hunters have built screen boxes which protect the hung carcass from the flies until it can be carried to the cooling room — which should be as quickly as possible.

When these screen boxes are not available, hunters often cover the meat with cotton gauze, or hang it in a gauze bag. Tightly fitted gauze is not as effective as that which hangs away from the carcass, for the flies can still get to the meat where the fabric touches it.

One of the best deterrents I know is black pepper. When going to deer woods I always carry a big quarter-pound can of black pepper. Over the years this has proven the best insect repellent that still keeps the meat palatable. Whether I'm going to haul out my game immediately or come back later, I give all exposed parts of the dressed animal a good dusting of pepper. This works equally well on all game.

In reasonably cold weather, of course, there is no problem with flies or other insects. The main idea is to cool the meat. This is done, as I have shown, by field-dressing as soon as possible after the kill. With larger game animals, where pack horses or other suitable transportation is involved, the meat is left to be quartered and hauled out the next day.

The one occasion I remember when this was not feasible was on Lac Seul in western Ontario. The week before Christmas that year, the thermometer dropped to 45-degrees below zero and stuck there during the whole period I was on a hunt for moose, with Bill Bousfield and Percy King.

On that trip we took three big bulls. We didn't stop at merely field-dressing them, but quartered the animals as soon as they had been gutted. The next day I learned why. Every one of those chunks of meat had frozen as solid as a block of granite.

Almost without exception, the big-game guides with whom I've hunted left the hide on the quarters to protect the meat from dirt, grass and leaves that would have to be cleaned off later as well as from the sweaty odor of the pack horses. Even with this hide on, most guides carry along a tarp that they use as a ground cover and as a wrap for the meat before it is placed in or on the pack saddle.

TRANSPORTING THE CARCASS

Since the meat poundage of big-game often runs well into three figures, two horses are usually needed to bring the animal out of the woods. Here a quarter may be placed in each pack saddle and the head and remainder of the carcass mounted on top. Except for the antlers, everything is covered with a tarp and lashed in place with ropes. The antlers top the load. We didn't have horses at Lac Seul, so we pulled our meat out of the brush on a sled, over rough logging trails.

I learned how valuable pack horses are the fall Jim Gay and I bagged an elk in one of the immense valleys of the Shirley Range, north of Medicine Bow in central Wyoming. The nearest point to which Jim could bring his four-wheel drive was on top of the ridge more than a mile and at least a thousand feet above our kill—a most conservative estimate. We brought those hams, shoulders, head and other parts out on a pack board. Every step of the way, I felt as though I were finishing a four-minute mile.

That wasn't the most rugged trip I ever made by packboard, however. We'd taken a Dall sheep in a part of Alaska's Talkeetna range in country so rugged that a pack horse would have needed feet like a mountain goat to get there. The guide and I brought out a ram carcass and head on two packboards. This took us the better part of a day.

One of the most unusual packing-out treks I've made was with Jim Gay and Chuck Czekula, both of Laramie, Wyoming. We were hunting the Platte Ridge in the southern part of the state. Jim downed a bull on the far side of the ridge, about three miles across rugged terrain from where our camp was located on the road. Chuck had brought a motor bike into camp

Packhorses provide an easy way of transporting big game. Here the guides lash sets of antlers atop a manta that covers a hide-on quarter of meat.

to save long walks on the ridgetop road. So someone suggested that we use the bike to get Jim's elk out.

This was easier said than done. We took a most zigzag course through the timber, going around windfalls, cutting logs here and there to make the route passable. After some hours, we finally got the motor bike to a point of ridge several hundred yards above the canyon where Jim had put the bullet into his elk. We packed the parts of the animal uphill on our shoulders, and Chuck brought out each piece strapped on the seat behind him.

There is much less rugged big-game country where one may go right to his kill by four-wheel drive. Usually that makes it easier but not always. We were in Arizona's Coconino National Forest with Jay Cravens, Forest Ranger there. I was shooting open sights on my old Krag .30-40 and got a glimpse of this elk with the biggest antler I had ever seen on a bull. When he went down I knew I had a world record, and I'm sure that antler had close to top measurements. The trouble was that he had only one, with a smooth knob where the other was supposed to be.

We killed the bull at the head of a long, flat meadow spotted with trees and close to a forest service road at the lower end. We walked back three or four miles to where we'd parked the jeep and drove it to the elk. With his block and tackle, Jay pulled the bull into a tree, drove the jeep under it and we let the carcass down to lie across the hood. The animal's body was so huge, the forester couldn't see over it from the driver's seat, so I had to pick our route out by walking in front of the vehicle and holding up a long stick with my handkerchief tied at the top.

We almost made it. Just as we entered the forest service road, the jeep hit a bump and the front wheels simply folded under it. We got out, built a fire, ate some emergency rations the forester carried and stayed there until Alan Watkins and my wife Kayte found us later in the evening.

That was the biggest bull elk I ever killed. When we put the quarters on the scales in the meat house, Jay figured that the live elk must have weighed close to a thousand pounds—even without his second horn, and Number 2 testicle, which was also missing.

With the smaller hoofed animals, getting the meat out of the woods is not nearly so onerous a chore. Sometimes you can pick up an antelope or javelina under one arm, and handle most of the smaller deer in that manner, though I've collected some mule deer bucks big enough to make me glad we had a pack string along.

Since by far the largest percentage of big-game animals brought out of the woods each year are whitetail deer, and since many of the methods of transportation may be applied to other creatures of approximately the same size, the discussion here will be centered around the whitetail, although much has already been written on the subject.

I learned the easiest way to get a buck from where it was downed to camp, or to mechanical transportation, some years ago from a city slicker who came up to hunt in north Georgia's Blue Ridge Mountains. I was camped on Noontootla Creek with a group of fellows who hunted early and late and usually spent the noonday hours in camp. We were there one day, munching on sandwiches, when this fellow came up the trail and stopped by our campfire.

"Boy!" he said. "I just shot down the biggest buck anyone ever saw in these woods. There's no way for me to get it out alone, so I had to come for some help."

"Where is he?" someone wanted to know.

"On the second ridge from here," the guy said, "and it's rough country."

Three of us volunteered to go with him and give him a hand. It took us almost an hour to reach the deer. It was a magnificent buck and every man in our bunch drooled. The hunter had gutted his deer nicely. We stood around a moment, admiring the antlers and the job of dressing.

"Fellows," he said, "I've had a hard day. I got up at 3:00 o'clock this morning, drove up here and climbed mountains till I'm plumb tuckered. So if you will bring my deer out to your camp, I'll sure be much obliged."

He put his rifle sling over his shoulder, said "I'll see you in camp," and took off down the mountain. We stared after him, then looked at one another and laughed.

"Well that does beat all," one of my partners said.

We talked it over and finally decided to haul the guy's deer out. This we did by stringing it between two poles and taking turns. The fellow did thank us, but never even offered us a piece of venison.

Those two poles are an excellent arrangement for man-handling deer in the woods. Possibly they are not the best under many circumstances, and certainly not the most common device. The average hunter prefers to drag his deer, and can handle a sizable animal if the going is not uphill.

When we hunted the Warwoman area in north Georgia with muzzle loaders a couple of seasons ago, Jack Crockford killed a medium buck a hundred yards down the far side of a ridge from camp. Howard Verner and I went back with him for pictures and to help him get the buck up the steep slope and across the long mountainside to camp. Howard always carried a small block and tackle in his pack, and with this we had no difficulty in skidding the buck up the mountain. Dragging the buck by hand from the ridge crest into the valley was little more than effortless.

Believe it or not, I once came on a pair of hunters pulling their deceased buck by the hind legs. This appeared somewhat of a chore, since the antlers caught on every other bush and the hair resisted skidding somewhat. I thought of the old classic where a veteran found two novice nimrods pulling a deer from the wrong end, and pointed out that dragging by the antlers would be easier. The two hunters changed ends and after they'd pulled a while, one of them stopped. "This is easier," he admitted, "but we're getting farther from the truck by draggin' this end."

By holding the antlers slightly off the ground, a hunter finds little trouble in skidding an average buck through the woods. Sometimes he can make this chore even less difficult by fastening a rope around the antlers and dragging with the rope over his shoulder. Most of a deer's weight is forward, and the rope helps hold a part of the body off the ground. One of my outdoor partners, Doctor Bob Hines, wears a belt much too wide to go through the loops of his trousers, but it has a purpose. He affixes ropes to it, turns the wide part forward and uses it for pulling out his deer or boar.

One pole works, above, but two would distribute the weight better and eliminate swing. Blaze-orange streamers or red cloth tied to the carcass would reduce the hazard of drawing fire from itchy hunters. Below, Jim Gay grips the antlers and then hauls. This method gets some of the weight off the ground and keeps the antlers from hanging up on brush or other obstacles.

If you must shoulder a deer, at least attach blaze-orange streamers to lessen the chance that it will acquire more bullet holes.

Two men, one on each side, make the job even easier. For a large animal, a stick tied close to the base of the antlers—or to the snout, if it's a boar— allows the head to be lifted far enough above the ground and picks up on the forequarters enough to make the skidding easier.

I have brought a number of smaller deer out on my shoulders. There are several ways to do this and all are dangerous if the woods is full of hunters and if you don't take the proper precautions. If the animal is within my load limit, I simply tie its front and hind feet together, attach a blaze orange cloth to the antlers, and drape the deer around my neck. The animal has been gutted and I'm likely to come in with a bloody coat unless I carry along a piece of plastic or a cloth to help soak up the blood.

Another way to backpack your deer is to make a "packsack" out of the carcass. I learned this from Ray Ward when T. C. Kennon, the custom rifle maker, and I hunted with Ray near Eagle Pass in Texas. Ray and I were in two tree stands a couple of hundred yards apart when I heard one shot late in the afternoon. I went over to help pack out his buck.

"I can do it better alone," he said, "if you'll carry my rifle."

I watched the operation, which was new to me. We didn't have a cord to tie the feet together, so Ray slit the skin on each hind leg to expose the big tendons. Those he pulled loose enough to force the foreleg back through that hind leg on the same side of the deer. He pulled each foreleg past its knee joint through the tendons, then to make certain they would hold, punched a hole in each foreleg below the knee joint and pushed through a small, stout peg to hold the legs in place.

I helped Ray lift the deer high enough so that the hindquarters were about the height of his shoulders and most of the buck's weight was balanced above his shoulders. The rack hung down in front, and this Ray held down with one hand to keep the carcass riding high.

Had I not been there to help, Ray says he would have raised the buck to a sitting position, sat down between the hind legs and put his arms through each loop formed by a fore and back leg. Then Ray would have rolled over and got to his feet from his knees. Ray said that another way would be to throw a rope over a limb and pull the buck high enough off the ground for Ray to slide his arms into the loops before releasing the rope secured to the limb. With this backpack carry Ray brought his animal easily to camp, about 1½ miles across a cactus flat.

I've never tried one method recommended by the experts. They call it the "rump pack." With this the hunter skins the hide off all four legs below the knee joints. He then cuts through the tendons at the front of each knee joint and breaks off the legs at the joint, leaving the loose flaps of skin. With these he ties the two front legs and then the two back legs together with square knots, pulling the joints as closely together as possible. This gives him two shoulder straps, both long enough so that the carcass rides at or close to the belt line, its weight hanging by the shoulder straps. The head hangs down and must be literally "carried" in one hand, or tied high and around in front to keep it out of the brush.

Where the country is rough and the brush high, experienced buck slayers who hunt in pairs or more, often use the pole carry, with the deer tied on one or two poles, high enough to keep it above the vegetation. The two-pole carry is more satisfactory, since it eliminates a lot of swing and distributes the weight to four shoulders instead of two. The higher the buck is tied between two poles, the less swing and the easier the chore of bringing it out.

One hunter I knew swore by the old Indian travois. He laid two ten- to twelve-foot poles parallel and about four feet apart on the ground. Three or four feet from the front end he lashed a pole between the two parallel bars and another about three feet behind that. Then he crossed two more poles between the diagonal corners to strengthen the contraption and serve as a brace. He pulled his deer far enough up on the crude travois so that when he picked up the front end, most of the heaviest part of the animal's body was off the ground, making the deer easier to drag. The hunter had to admit, however, that this worked best on level ground or on a downhill course.

Jim Gay demonstrated the most picturesque way I've ever seen of getting a deer down a long mountain. Bill Rae and I were hunting mule deer with Jim in western Wyoming. The snow was about two feet deep, so Jim simply handed his rifle to me, rolled the buck over on its back, picked up the head, straddled the carcass and rode it down the mountain as if it were a sled. Jim, on the buck, slid down about four times as fast as Bill and I could walk behind him, and he didn't take more than a couple of spills, either. Once when his "sled" came to a jarring halt against a snow-covered boulder and another time it got tangled in some brush.

Of course the easiest way, if you are hunting from a horse, is to bring out your smaller kill — such as a buck — draped over a saddle, as Cotton Watkins and I did in southwest Colorado. When we had half a dozen miles of rugged mountain trail to negotiate between the top of the mesa and the ranch, we tied the buck down securely to make certain that the sharp hoofs or antlers did not spur the horse. We walked down the trail leading the horse. It was certainly convenient to walk out and let our saddle horse do the work.

If you are fortunate enough to make a kill where you can bring your car to it or close, and if the carcass has any heat left in it, don't throw it in your car trunk and close down the lid. The meat must have plenty of ventilation, especially if you have a considerable distance to drive.

SKINNING

You can get a number of opinions on the proper time to skin a deer, and I suppose this applies to other big game as well. The time for skinning ranges all the way from immediately after the animal is gutted until just before it's cut into edible portions for packaging. Some nimrods I know pack cheesecloth into the woods, and skin and quarter their game on the spot, wrapping the meat in the fabric before it is packed out. Others skin the carcass at camp or at home before turning it over to the butcher or freezer-locker plant for curing.

Emory Willis, my favorite deer-hunting butcher, tells me that the time to skin any game animal is immediately before the final processing. From the time it is killed until the butchering, it should hang in temperatures ranging somewhere between 36 and 40 degrees. If the atmospheric temperature is right and reasonably constant, this hanging can be done in camp, or at home, but the best bet is the cooling room at the locker plant. How long the meat cures depends on its condition. A young animal loaded with fat may not need more than ten days in the cooler. A lean, stringy old one may need thirty days or more to bring it to its maximum tenderness. Willis tells me that a sort of hard and dark crust may form on meat cured with the hide off. This doesn't hurt the meat underneath, but the crust must be trimmed away and that portion is lost. A hide-on carcass matures more evenly and with better results.

I must admit that my butcher does a better job of skinning out a game animal than I do. But I've taken the hide off many a critter, including my share of whitetail and mule deer bucks. I'm sure the easiest and simplest way to disrobe a deer carcass in the field was outlined for me by Dr. Charles Marshall, a teaching conservationist who served his time with the Georgia Game and Fish Commission. Charlie says you do it with a *golf ball.*

Where you start such an unorthodox peeling process depends on whether you have removed the scalp for making a shoulder mount of the head. But from any point, the procedure and result are the same.

Says Marshall: "After you field-dress the deer by conventional methods, remove the front legs by cutting through the 'knee' joint. The rear legs are cut at the hock. Split the skin on the inside of each leg. If you are *not* going to mount the head, split the hide (which is already open from vent to brisket) from the rib cage to the lower jaw. Cut the skin around the upper neck joint behind the ears. Carefully remove the hide from approximately eight inches of the neck. Tie a rope or chain around the deer's neck and attach it to a stout limb. Or if you prefer not to lift the carcass this high, tie it to a nearby tree.

"Now for the golf ball. Insert the golf ball (a small round stone will do) about four inches under the skin on the back of the neck. Tie one end of a stout rope around the skin-covered ball and the other to an automobile or truck. Drive the vehicle away, and the skin will rapidly separate from the carcass.

"Your last step is to remove the head and tail. A clean cloth wrapped around the meat will keep insects and dirt off the carcass during transportation to the locker."

I've never tried the golf ball or round stone method but Charlie Marshall assured me that the skin comes off clean, with a minimum amount of meat so that very little fleshing is needed.

Over half a century or more, all of the skinning I've done has been with a knife in the orthodox manner—*a la* mountain man and swamper before the auto came along. I suppose we could have done the power peeling with a horse, except that we usually brought our game out of the back country with the hide on and never undressed the carcass until it had been properly cured and was ready to be butchered. Then we went about the skinning job in a leisurely manner and rather enjoyed it.

This particular step in preparing most hoofed big-game animals for the

To employ the golf-ball skinning technique, first cut off the front legs at the knee joint and the hind legs at the hock. Then split the hide up the middle of each leg. (The animal has been field-dressed and split up the brisket.) Peel the neck skin back. Then insert a golf ball or round stone so that you can tie a rope around the skin-covered bulb it forms. Attach the other end of the rope to your vehicle, and drive away. That's it.

larder follows approximately my old procedure. I say *most*, because there are exceptions. If no trophy is involved and you want a wild boar or javelina for meat, it may be treated with boiling water, without being skinned, as with a domestic pig. In several instances we have used a fifty-gallon clean steel drum, set high enough on rocks or concrete blocks so that we could build a fire under and around it. When the water boils, dip the animal one end at the time until the hair is loose and slides easily off the skin. If the boar is so large that two men can't handle it comfortably, you can place the fire and drum under a large tree limb. Then you can do the job with a small block and tackle. There should be a clean table or heavy boards to lay the boar on for hair removal.

The only difference between a wild and domestic boar is the time between killing and processing in the above manner. The domestics are killed, bled and dipped within a relatively short period. Game animals must often be carted long distances out of the woods. Thus the hair tends to set and may be a bit more difficult to remove. Also you are treating a field-dressed animal.

Most hunters find it simpler to skin a boar as they would any other game animal, but those who use the boiling water treatment claim that leaving the skin and fat under it makes a better piece of meat.

The steps in skinning most hoofed animals are about the same and again the deer is a good example. No matter how you go about it, skinning is a rather simple chore, if you follow certain fundamentals.

Of course you need a sharp knife that will hold an edge, and the four- or five-inch blade used for field-dressing is as good as any.

You must hang the deer. I've watched hunters skin them with head up and head down and do a creditable job both ways. I prefer that my buck be hung by the hind legs. To place him in the proper position, I cut off all four legs at the "knee" joints. Then I cut through the skin above the hind leg joints and pull slack into the big tendons there. Into each of these loops I insert and tie a rope and pull the carcass up to a limb or other horizontal support, high enough so that I may comfortably reach the leg ends.

Some hunters I know hang a deer by one leg while they skin out the other, and then switch. After the hide has been pulled down on both hams, they fasten both legs to keep the animal steady and secure through the remainder of the job.

I prefer to tie up the ends of both hind legs before I start. I split each from near the base of the tail to the top of the joint. Then I open the skin on the inside of the forelegs from the brisket. I peel the skin of each leg from around the hindquarters and shoulders, using my knife to help separate the inside skin from the meat, where pulling it free is difficult.

At this point, if I want to save the tail, I make a lengthwise cut on the underside, about half way to the end of the tailbone. This gives me room enough to pull the skin loose around the base of the tail, where I can get a grip and yank out the tailbone.

From this point on, stripping off the hide is mainly a matter of strength. The job is easier when the skin is pulled straight down off the body. Where its hold is tenacious, I pound the skin loose with my fist. Sometimes I need a knife blade to cut the tough tissue in the more stubborn places. I skin to the edge of where the cape has been removed, or to the head if there is to be no cape.

I've seen guys hack off the head with axes and otherwise butcher the neck meat, which is excellent for stew meat or jerky. This hacking is entirely unnecessary. I separate the skull from the atlas joint (first vertebra) by first cutting through the neck meat to the joint, all the way around the neck. Then I can easily twist the head and lift it off.

SKINNING

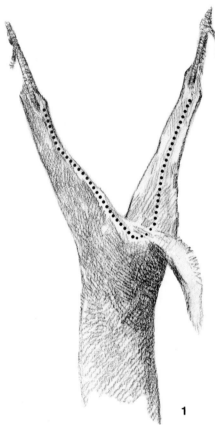

Insert ropes through cuts between the bone and tendon above the hock. Hang the carcass at a comfortable working height. Then split the skin at the base of the tail and up both hindquarters.

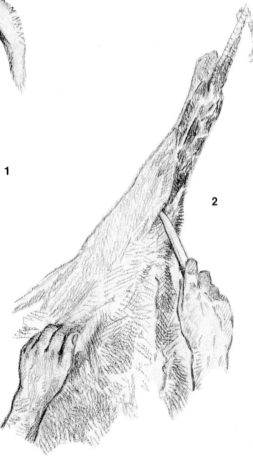

Cut and peel the skin on each hindquarter back to the tail. Then cut lengthwise up the tail's underside halfway to the end of the tailbone.

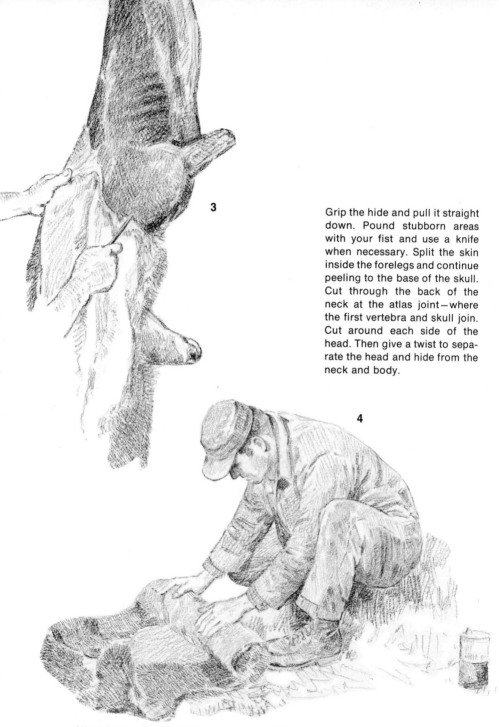

3

Grip the hide and pull it straight down. Pound stubborn areas with your fist and use a knife when necessary. Split the skin inside the forelegs and continue peeling to the base of the skull. Cut through the back of the neck at the atlas joint—where the first vertebra and skull join. Cut around each side of the head. Then give a twist to separate the head and hide from the neck and body.

4

Allow the thoroughly fleshed and salted hide to air dry and drain in a cool place for about 24 hours. For shipment to a tanner, the hide should be rolled and placed in a protective wrap such as burlap so that it can breathe.

FIELD CARE OF THE HIDE

Most hunters prefer to save deer hides that can be made into buckskins, which have many uses: gloves, moccasins, shirts, jackets, or pocketbooks. So while you've got it in your hands — provided that it's skinned clean with no meat or fat left on — spread the hide out on a smooth surface and rub it down with salt. The amount of salt you'll need depends on the size of the hide. But as a rule of thumb, a pound box of table salt will do the job for an average skin. The salt must be distributed evenly over the inside of the hide and rubbed in with the palm and heel of your hand. Don't spare the pressure. And, cover every inch of skin.

The essential thing in preserving a trophy or hide is to skin it clean, or "flesh" it well, as soon as possible to help prevent decay. Even salt won't penetrate gobs of fat and meat soon enough. Nor will it get far enough into folds in the skin.

Salt draws out moisture. So to prevent sloppiness in transportation or shipping, it is best to spread the hide out flat for 24 hours or so to allow this moisture to drain off or evaporate. Then roll up the hide and store it in a cool place for later mailing to your taxidermist, who knows the best tanners.

Where no salt is available, the hide — thoroughly fleshed — is often tacked up to air dry, but makes for more awkward handling through the parcel services. The large, air-dried hide is best rolled for shipment.

TANNING AT HOME

If you are a do-it-yourselfer and want to go all the way and make your own buckskin, there are several methods, but whichever you choose, prepare yourself for a bit of physical effort.

Briefly, the tanning process means scraping all meat and fat from the flesh side of the skin and removing the hair from the outside. Then comes soaking and stretching the skin to break down the fibers. Finally, you must smoke the hide to toughen it, close the pores, color it, and make it a useable piece of leather.

A simple procedure is to soak the green hide for a day or two in a water solution before stretching it and scraping off all surplus flesh from the inside. The skin is then soaked again until the hair loosens. To hasten this, especially for the skins of larger animals, the frontiersmen used a weak solution of lye water which they made by filtering water through hickory ashes. Today you can buy caustic potash or potassium hydroxide for this purpose at the drugstore. These chemicals are powerful and will eat up a skin unless converted into a weak solution of lye water — between five and ten percent chemical. With this solution you must watch the skin daily until the hair begins to slip.

Another recommended solution consists of two gallons of water, one quart of slaked lime and one quart of wood ashes. The skin is then soaked for 24 hours or until the hair slips and can be pulled out.

TANNING

To begin the tanning process, soak the green hide for a day or so to loosen surplus flesh. Then scrape this excess away. Later, soak the hide again in a special solution until the hair loosens. Then stretch the hide over a board or log and pull or scrape off all hair, as shown.

After rinsing the hide to remove chemicals and further tidying it up, moisten it and work it over a board or carpenter's sawhorse until pliable. Then oil and smoke it.

Some experts do not recommend lye water for the lighter skins, but give them a longer soaking in salt and alum water, stirring daily until the hair is loose. With this solution there is less chance of ruining a skin.

At the end of the soaking period, stretch the hide tightly, hair side out, over a log or on a board and scrape off all hair with a dull instrument. The Indians used flint and sometimes a large mussel shell. The pioneers used an adze or short tool made like a hoe. Sometimes they used the back of a hunting or kitchen knife.

With the hair off, rinse the hide thoroughly to get out all lye, salt, alum or whatever. Then hang the skin for a few hours to let it drain. Check it again for any surplus flesh and especially thick places which should be scraped to the thinness of the surrounding hide. This operation is a painstaking one.

Now is the time to break down the fibers and soften the hide. Next pull, stretch, twist and rub the skin over a fixed plank or board until it becomes pliable. (A carpenter's sawhorse, with horizontal plank worn smooth, is good for this.) During this process keep the hide moist but not wet.

Some of the home buckskin makers say it's best to oil the hide before the stretching starts. Others work in the oil or grease as the softening progresses. For this the Indians used the "brains" of the animal, dissolving them in water by simmering them over a slow fire until the lumps could be worked out with the fingers and the concoction made into a paste. This they rubbed into the skin's outside.

The more modern method is to oil the hide with neat's-foot or cottonseed oil, or even lard rendered from suet. After the oiling, the skin is again worked until it is as soft as chamois skin, and will no longer harden after a soaking. The man who makes a buckskin on his own, earns it.

To complete the job, smoke the hide over a "cold" fire of green oak or hickory. The Indians did this by building their fire in a hole in the ground, with the skin stretched on a frame above it, making a sort of tepee. The fire must be tended carefully to keep smoke only and no flame. This smoking finishes the type of buckskin you will value as one of your trophies, whether it ends up as a pair of gloves, moccasins or part of a jacket.

5

Preparing and Preserving the Meat

IT'S NOT LAZINESS, for I consider myself a rather ardent member of the do-it-yourself cult, but I go along with the group who think that the most proficient way to convert the carcass of the big-game animal into roasts, chops and what-have-you is to turn it over to a processing plant or to a local butcher. Usually the cost of this job is nominal, and the results better than when an amateur, such as I, attempts to do it.

Meat processing costs appear to vary from one section of the country to another. Our local butcher, Emory Willis and his son Ken, process over 200 deer a season. For skinning (where necessary), cutting into edible portions, wrapping and freezing, his overall charge has been fifteen cents a pound. Emory charges based on the total weight of the carcass brought to his plant.

Having someone else butcher your game animal for you is not without its pitfalls. On more than one occasion, when I turned my elk over to a processing plant in a western town, I got a solemn promise that they would hang it for three weeks before butchering, I'm sure they threw it on a table and started cutting before I was well out the front door. Once my box of frozen meat got home the day after I did. And then there was that time when my meat came to me as bologna instead of the expected steaks, chops and roasts.

AGING

Proper aging, as we have seen, is important. The best piece of venison we ever had at our house was one that came within a fraction of spoiling. My hunting partner and I divided a young buck I'd been lucky enough to bag while we were on a hunt. I settled for the loin and gave him the rest of the meat. Instead of hanging the loin to age, I placed it in a second refrigerator we keep for surplus food stuffs. The meat was snug up against the refrigerator wall and, after a couple of days, was beginning to freeze around the edges. Too cold, meat doesn't cure properly. Since the temperature outside the box was only in the high 30s, I laid the loin out. When we went out of town a few days later for a two week trip, I forgot about tending to the loin. While we were away, the temperature climbed into the high 60s.

That chunk of meat was the first thing I thought of when I got home. It had a tainted smell and felt a bit slick, so I was certain I'd lost it. But to make sure, I carried it to my butcher. He felt and smelled it and said, "I think we can make it edible."

While I looked on, he washed it down with vinegar. This removed both the slickness and odor.

"A meat market would go out of business without vinegar," he confided.

Whatever had happened to that loin was just right. The chops were tasty and so tender that we could cut them with a fork. I don't, however, recommend such a procedure for curing meat. It's best to let it hang in the optimum temperature for the right length of time.

Steaks and ribs broiled over an open fire help ease the pain of roughing it.

After meat has aged properly, you must decide whether you want it butchered by a professional or whether you do the job yourself. For several reasons, some hunters prefer to cut up their own wild meat. They say that where the job is done in a processing plant, on a wholesale basis, the meat often lacks the proper care and attention. The meat may not be thoroughly cleaned of hair, dirt or other foreign matter. Where so many carcasses are handled, your young, tender buck or bull or boar may get mixed up with a tough, stringy one.

Where to do this job? The poorest place to butcher is in the woods, or in camp. I have bagged game, however, in spots so rugged that it really seemed simpler to build a shelter and stay there until I'd eaten all that meat, rather than try to bring it out. The whole or quartered carcass is more practical to pack out than the butchered parts. There are exceptions to this. Once in the far northern Yukon, we ate our meat from the trophies we killed. In thirty days the amount we consumed was prodigious. After many years I still remember those steaks and ribs of caribou, sheep and moose broiled over a campfire.

Some eastern nimrods who hunt in the West go in campers or pickup trucks and bring their meat home with them. Others have it processed and shipped. The first time I ever dealt with a locker plant in a far corner of the continent, I was worried about whether I'd ever see my meat. But in over forty years I've never had any trouble on that score.

Twenty-five or more years ago, the express agencies used what was known as a "church box," a large insulated container in which the meat was packed with a sufficient amount of dry ice to bring it frozen solid across the continent. Then came heavy cardboard boxes, which I don't consider as foolproof as those old church boxes, but they normally bring the meat in reasonably good shape.

BUTCHERING

If you decide to butcher your own game, there are a number of things you should consider. First are the tools. To do the proper job, you should have a long butcher knife, a shorter boning knife, a meat cleaver and a saw. A hacksaw is all right, but a butcher's saw is better, if you can find one. You might even want meat hooks, but most amateurs use a gambrel stick that is long enough to hold the hind legs far enough apart for easy operation. A stout table is an asset.

You need a place in which to hang your animal high enough to allow you to start at one end and split the carcass down the center of the backbone, into halves. The saw is necessary for a careful, precise cut. Some fellows I know use the basement for hanging and others the woodshed, but what you need is any place with stout beams to eliminate danger of your meat's slipping or pulling free and falling.

BUTCHERING

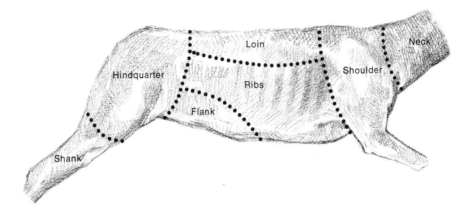

The top drawing shows basic cuts. The bottom notes favored uses.

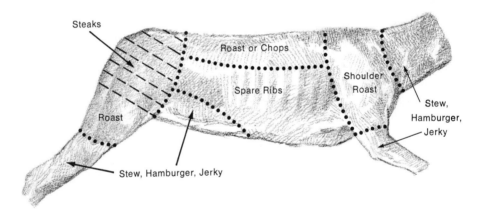

If your animal is large enough and not already quartered for its trip out of the woods, you may need to cut off the legs and then split the carcass in half for easy handling. Emory Willis claims that with the average deer or antelope, this halving is not necessary and that the carcass is as easily worked when laid whole on the table. He admits, however, that the meat is cut up about the same way, whether whole or halved.

"What are the steps?" I asked.

"First of all," he said, "we hang the skinned animal and hose it down to get off all the hair, dirt, grass, pine straw or whatever, then wipe it clean with a vinegar-soaked cloth and allow it to drain."

"Some of the experts say that water hurts the meat," I pointed out.

"Not at all," he disagreed. "I've washed a thousand."

Here is Emory's procedure: After removing the surplus fat, he moves the whole carcass to the cutting table and lays it on its side for separation into the basic pieces: shoulders, hindquarters, loin, ribs, flank and neck. He uses the saw or cleaver where necessary to cut through bone and separate the pieces.

Before dismemberment, some butchers split the carcass in half by sawing down the middle of the backbone, leaving two separate halves. Willis thinks it's easier to work with the carcass in one piece instead of two.

He cut the neck off just where it joins the shoulders. He finds this first cut easier to make while the carcass is whole. Willis then cuts off the front part of the deer, immediately behind the shoulders. Then he spreads the two forequarters and separates them by sawing down the middle of the backbone.

Willis removes the hindquarters next. He cuts these loose from the back of the flank to a point on the backbone about four inches from the base of the tail. It's best to use a saw to cut through the backbone and then to split the two quarters apart.

The remaining middle section—with its loins, ribs and flanks—may be split by sawing or chopping down the middle of the backbone. You can then cut off the flank meat and separate the loin from the ribs on each piece.

This leaves the basic pieces to be cut, chopped and sawed into the proper cuts.

Some of Willis's customers like steaks out of a part of the shoulder, but unless otherwise instructed, Willis cuts the upper shoulder into three roasts. The lower shoulder, or shank, may also be made into a roast or cut into chunks for stew meat or hamburger.

Some prefer the top section of the hindquarter as a rump roast. On larger game animals this may work out, but on a deer Willis considers this top section too small a piece of meat for a roast. He recommends that this entire quarter be cut into round steaks. Thickness of the steaks is a matter of personal preference, but they are usually sliced about 1 to 1½ inches thick. I like mine a bit thicker than that. The lower part of the hindquarter, or shank, makes good stew or hamburger meat.

The loin and ribs have already been split and separated. Some hunters may prefer to cut the long strip of loin muscle into roasts, but most people I know want it in chops, claiming that it is tastier and more tender than any meat on a game animal. The chops are made by cutting down through the meat to the backbone, then chopping through the bone with a cleaver. If your aim is poor, you'd better pound the cleaver through with a maul.

While that cleaver is still in your hand, chop the ribs for cooking by cutting across the rib case to make long strips about three or four inches wide. Each strip should be made into approximate squares by cutting through the meat between the rib bones.

Willis removes the layer of neck meat by slicing the neck lengthwise down to the spinal column, then cutting the meat from around the spine as if he were taking off a layer of heavy skin. The neck meat is good for stew, hamburger or jerky, as is the flank, or the layer between the back of the ribs and the hindquarter.

The butchering job outlined above is predicated on a perfect carcass, with no bullet holes, and no bloodshot or tainted meat—which is seldom the case unless an animal is shot in the upper neck or head. Close to a hundred percent of kills have meat which is bloodshot, including those where the bullet breaks the lower neck and leaves pulverized bone there. Many times high-powered bullets through the shoulder, hindquarters or along the back mess up a carcass considerably. Sometimes where this meat is not properly handled, parts of it may become tainted and smelly. Most of the experts who write about butchering animals claim that all such flesh should be cut out and discarded.

Willis disagrees with this. It's not wise to take chances with the tainted meat, of course, but the bloodshot portions can be treated and made palatable. Willis says that a bullet through solid meat tears up the blood vessels and causes the tiny veins to clot with blood. Most of the time these bloody portions can be cut away and soaked in cold water until the blood is washed out. Then it cannot be distinguished from the other meat.

Scraps left along the bone from boning and other discarded portions of the carcass often make a good pile of meat for use in stews, soups and hamburger. Another delicious edible portion is the brain. You may frown on the idea of eating "brains" but not after you have tried them. They are a delicacy, comparable to pig and calf brains. Kenneth Willis, Emory's son, who helps him butcher deer each season, collects and freezes the brains that the hunters don't want and "puts up" enough to last him most of the year. Many hunters also pass up the liver, heart and kidneys, but seldom again after they have tried these portions.

What might be called the by-products of a big-game carcass are such edibles as sausage, bologna, burgers, stew, and smoked or dried pieces. One of the products we enjoyed was elkburgers. We did not consider it sacrilege that we ground our elk scraps and some of the larger chunks, too, with an equal amount of beef and froze them as five-ounce patties, which could be taken out of the freezer and put directly into the skillet for a quick meal. This idea is not original with us. Willis tells me that many of his deer customers have parts of their venison ground with beef or pork or a combination, and seasoned as sausage or burgers, according to the specifications of his customers.

In this regard, one of the worst mistakes an amateur butcher can make — and he has to be a real tyro to do this — is to cut meat *with* the grain. When the tough tendons run along a strip or chunk of meat, it chews like a piece of rawhide. All meat should be sliced *across* the grain.

PRESERVING AND STORAGE

Now that you've got your meat separated into the proper edible portions, it is obvious that you won't be able to eat it all in one or two sittings, so your next step is preserving it for many delicious meals ahead. Today, most of it will be wrapped, labeled, and frozen and then held in the deep-freezer until ready for use.

Outside the polar regions, the deep-freezer is comparatively new as a means of preserving foods. But the freezer's reliability is threatened by power failures and natural or man-caused disasters. To me, it is unfortunate that human survival is often based on such a frail thing as electric power.

There is challenge, fun, and satisfaction in going back to the pioneer ways and preserving at least a portion of our meat without the assistance of late twentieth century devices.

Brine Cure

The pioneers had a number of ways of curing and otherwise saving their wild meat. They used one procedure that, with our freezing units, we don't need today. They made deer "hams" just as they salt-cured hog hams. They used both the wet and dry methods.

For every hundred pounds of meat, the brine method required 8 pounds of salt, 2 pounds of sugar, and 2 ounces of saltpeter dissolved in each 5 to 6 gallons of water. The hams and shoulders were fitted loosely into a barrel or crock and covered with this cold brine. Usually they were shifted and repacked in the same brine on the fifth, fifteenth and thirtieth day, if they were large enough to remain covered more than a month.

Now, as then, the meat should soak four days to the pound. If the scum of white mold on top of the brine becomes syrupy or hard before the time is up, the meat should be taken out and scrubbed with a brush and warm water and then repacked with new brine in a clean barrel. (Modern outfitters sometimes inject brine into the meat with a hypodermic-type pump.)

By the dry method, each ham or shoulder is packed in 7 to 8 pounds of salt, 1½ to 2 pounds of sugar and 2 ounces of saltpeter per 100 pounds of meat. To this sometimes is added a mixture of 2 ounces of red pepper, and 2 ounces of black pepper and brown sugar in various small amounts. Half of the required amount of these mixed ingredients should be thoroughly rubbed in the first day, with special attention to forcing the mixture into and around the top of the butt and hock. The other half should be rubbed in the third day and the tenth day—the meat "overhauled" with that portion of the mixture that has fallen off into the bottom of the storage barrel.

To make this concoction stick better, some of the old-timers stirred it up in honey or molasses when they had enough of one of these for the job.

Two days per pound was the accepted time for curing by the dry method, but a heavier piece of meat was often allowed to cure three to four weeks without harm. The hams were watched and "overhauled" when needed.

Smoking was usually the accepted climax of the salt-curing. At the end of the prescribed time the hams and shoulders were taken out of the salt and soaked in cold water for a couple of hours. Then they were washed thoroughly in warm water. They were hung eight to eleven feet high in the smokehouse without touching one another and allowed to drain for half a day before being smoked over a green hardwood, preferably hickory.

The idea in smoking is to produce smoke and no heat. Here the fire was tended to ensure that it did not flame after being built. Green wood or green hardwood sawdust kept the flames smothered. The smoking time was usually two or three days with the smokehouse temperature around 100-120 degrees, and longer if the inside temperature was lower.

The pioneers then smeared the cured dark meat with black pepper and sometimes sprinkled red pepper over it. Then they wrapped it in cloth or heavy paper for storage. They bound the meat tightly enough to seal it away from the air if possible. And to help with this they used a sealer of sticky flour paste. Wild meat cured and stored in this manner usually kept over long periods.

Jerky

In the early days of the West, jerky was an important food staple. Jerking meat was a simple method of preserving game meat so that it would keep for months and even years. It is possible that jerky was developed first in the hot, dry countries, since it could be made there by laying out strips of meat in the sun, where they lost moisture quickly without spoiling or being attacked by a variety of insects. The idea spread across North America, and now most deer hunters think about converting at least a portion of their venison into jerky—even if they never do it.

Jerky remains an emergency ration. It is concentrated calories, protein, vitamins and substance that keep men going. A month's supply can be packed into a very small space. When a man has jerky, he needs little else in the way of emergency food. When I'm hunting or fishing in the far back country, I keep a supply of jerky in my kit. The stuff would come in handy

Here a guide dries jerky with the aid of sun, air, and a "cold" wood fire. Regarding wood, the author recommends birch in north country and other hard, sweet wood available in the South.

if ever I got lost or caught with a broken leg. Not only that, but I often travel through the day with only a few strips of jerky and several handfuls of parched corn, which together make a perfect meal, calorie-and-vitamin-wise. It's rather restful to sit down and ruminate, physically as well as otherwise, over these two food items. The way a small portion can satisfy the hunger in a man is just short of amazing. And it's compact and light to pack.

Years ago my friend Horace Kephart, who was one of the early southern woodsmen to put his knowledge of woods lore and craft eloquently into words, told me that the word "jerky" was the North American translation of a Peruvian word "ccharqui," which meant meat cut into flakes and dried without salt. Our early westerners, the Indians among them, made their jerky by cutting the meat into thin, narrow strips and stringing it on small limbs or flat stones. The hot, arid wind and sun quickly dried it until it was as brittle as a chip. In some instances the drying process was speeded by a "cold" fire, preferably from birchwood, which also smoked the meat.

One later innovation was to soak the strips in a solution of salt water for a few hours, depending on the thickness, then sprinkle them lightly with black pepper before drying. This served two purpose: to flavor the meat and to keep off flies.

I must have cut my first teeth on jerky. I've chewed on it ever since I could remember. You don't eat it fast, but chew slowly until your saliva softens it and a fragment of meat becomes a mouthful. I've had jerky from most of the hoofed animals—some of it as thin as a wafer and other cut into thick strips. One of the most satisfying chunks of the stuff I ever ate was in the far corner of northwest Canada, after we had killed a moose. Our Indian guides cut strips about 1½ inches wide, one inch thick and seven to eight inches long and dried them on slender poles over a smoke. These strips weren't so crisp as the thinner jerky I had known and didn't appear very appetizing.

A couple of days later my guide and I stopped for lunch on a long mountain slope. The guide built a fire while I unwrapped my sandwich of boiled ham and cheese the camp cook had packed for me. Instead of eating, I watched the guide while he got two of those moose chunks out of his saddle bag, ran them through with a willow spit and toasted them quickly over the flames. Without a word, he handed one to me. I was frugal enough to carry my sandwich back to camp instead of throwing it to the wolves or whatever else might have found it. But from then on, the guide and I ate moose jerky every day for lunch.

If you really want to go modern on the jerky-making job, spread the thin meat strips on the rack of your electric oven, turn the temperature to "warm," or about 150 degrees and leave it until the strips are hard and dry. This usually takes anywhere from six to eight hours. Some hunters salt and pepper their meat before placing it in the oven and occasionally one will admit that he fancies up his jerky with a smidgen of barbecue sauce. Tastes vary from man to man.

Ground Meat

One of my mountain neighbors had an appealing way of storing a portion of his venison. He ground it up with an equal amount of hog meat and then cooked these hamburgers — or deerburgers — before putting them up for future use. After cooking, he packed the burgers in a wide-mouthed jar and covered them with fat he had rendered from beef suet. He claimed he could keep the meat this way for years without its spoiling, losing its taste, or becoming rancid. One thing for sure, I tried his burgers a few times and always found them tasty.

Stew

Not long ago Ken Willis presented me with a can of deer stew he had put up the season before. It was so delicious that I asked for his recipe so that I could pass it along as one of the choice ways of preserving part of the scrap meat from a big-game carcass. This recipe should work equally well with elk, caribou, moose and other such wild game. Here's how Ken puts up enough stew to provide his family with some of its most delectable meals:

Boil approximately 30 pounds of venison and remove any bones.

Put this once through chopper with large blade and pour this into a larger pot with a portion of the broth.

Next add 15 to 20 pounds of boiled *turkey tails*. (Here I asked if other parts of the turkey wouldn't be just as good or better, and Ken assured me it was the tail meat that gave his stew its special flavor. I further asked where the average man such as I, could buy turkey tails. He said any meat market would get them for me.) The boiled tails are boned, ground and added with some of the broth to the venison in the pot.

In succession Ken puts through the grinder and adds to his growing mixture the following: 12 to 15 pounds of onions, about 2 gallons of canned tomatoes (also ground) and 1½ gallons of sweet corn. Then he adds three or four pounds each of okra and lima beans.

To give all this a richer color and flavor, he pours in a half gallon to a gallon of tomato paste until the mixture tastes just right to him.

To thicken his stew, Ken grinds and adds 12 to 15 pounds of Irish or white potatoes. For seasoning he uses salt, red and cayenne pepper, 1 cup of sugar and then black pepper, which he puts in last. He uses no prescribed amount of salt and pepper, but seasons the stew to his taste.

All this must be cooked, and continuously stirred to keep the potatoes from sticking. Occasionally venison or turkey broth must be added to keep the stew from becoming too thick.

"That's not a very precise recipe," I said.

"It's not supposed to be," he assured me. "Sometimes I add other vegetables, or a rabbit or squirrel I happen to have in my freezer. My stew hardly ever turns out the same, but it's always good."

To that I could agree.

The nearby canning plant cans the stew for Ken, with the usual steam pressure treatment. The pressure cooking is recommended by all food experts. They say that the boiling water for home canning is not hot enough and that home-canned meat or stew might spoil.

Sometimes Ken cuts the ingredients down to a fraction of the big recipe and makes much smaller quantities, which he puts in cartons and quick-freezes. This, of course, is as good a method as any for preserving meat.

6

The Head Mount

ONE OF MY favorite friends and outdoor partners on many a big-game hunt in the Rocky Mountains is Jim Gay, of Laramie, Wyoming. A century or more ago he would have been one of the noted mountain men of his day, for he has all the qualifications of ruggedness, ingenuity and resourcefulness with which those who kept their hair and the rest of themselves intact were endowed. Even in these modern times, you could drop him into any wilderness — however remote — and wager your last flint and steel that he'd come out as healthy and unperturbed as when he went in.

All of my trips with Jim have been an education in how one should conduct himself in the outdoors for the most pleasure and success. Together we've been up against some pretty rugged situations, but my old partner's know-how always brought us through in peak condition.

Jim Gay's business is taxidermy. He has spent most of his life working at it. He served his apprenticeship with Jonas Brothers in Denver and then worked with that world-famous concern for some fifteen years before he went off to fight in World War II. He didn't go back with Jonas after the war but hung out his own shingle in Laramie. In the last quarter century the fame of Jim's shop has spread around the globe.

Taxidermy is by no means Jim's whole life. His reputation as a big-game outfitter and guide is known wherever hunters gather. When the cool September winds begin to blow through the high country, he turns his business over to his wife Esther, son Jimmy, and his staff and heads out for the boondocks to guide his clients for antelope, sheep, deer, elk or whatever. His territory extends beyond Wyoming and surrounding states. He has guided in Alaska — where his brother owns a flying service — for bear, moose, sheep and caribou. He has also been to Africa on a number of occasions, sometimes with hunting parties to take care of their trophies and other times to hunt with Esther, whose fascination for the outdoors is as complete as her husband's.

Jim sets aside two weeks out of each fall for what he calls his vacation.

Naturally, he goes hunting. I was fortunate enough to be invited on one of those hunts to Platte Ridge, a 9,000 foot height of land along the Colorado line. Being a fellow with an easily twisted gun arm, I accepted and this became one of my memorable hunting experiences.

I was with Jim, his son Jimmy, and a couple of fellows who work with them in the shop when we pitched our camp in a corner of that range where the trails run out. We found the country wild, rugged and picturesque. Much of it is plateau, forested with lodgepole pines — spindly ones that make up thickets and big old ones that make up open stands, full of wind-thrown timber. Forested slopes drop off into Douglas Creek on one side, but across the plateau are long, open points hanging a thousand feet above the sinuous Platte River. They are grassy and loaded with buck brush, a favorite food of the mule deer.

On the first morning of our hunt, Jim and I devoted our time to scouting for big tracks and fresh sign of both mule deer and elk so that we could concentrate on the most promising part of the range. Our long hike carried us down Platte Ridge, through timbered patches and into likely hollows.

We found abundant evidence that mule deer had been there, but the ground was dry and it was difficult to judge the age of the tracks. On our way back to camp, along one of the jeep trails, we came upon a tent occupied by three hunters. As we approached, Jim pointed out a tremendous six-point rack of an elk set up on an old stump.

"A beautiful head," I commented. Then I saw a glint in the guide's eyes.

"What's wrong with it?" I asked.

"The rack is one of the prettiest I've seen from this region," he agreed, "but they sure butchered it, if they want a trophy mount."

We examined the antlers carefully, and he showed me what he meant. Instead of caping out the animal and cutting off the proper portion of skull, they had chopped about a third of the skull away with an ax, leaving hide around the base of the antlers and making any kind of trophy mount, even with a new scalp, a very difficult task for the taxidermist.

"We get them in the shop like this many times," he said.

"Well then," I said, "just how should the head be skinned out and the skull prepared?"

"If we're lucky enough to get our sights in the proper place on a buck," he replied, "I'll show you."

I had more than one reason to anticipate my guide's promise to show me how to undress a trophy. I thought about this later while we covered the woods afoot. Even though I might have a guide to skin out my trophy, not all guides know the correct procedure of taking a cape. Then too, the majority of hunters don't even use a guide. I've known many an outdoorsman who killed his buck or bull when he was alone, far back in the woods. The only way he could bring the animal out was in quarters, on his back. In a few instances, the rack was a magnificent trophy.

Jim Gay, shown here, suggests taking close-up photos just like these. Details of head features later help the taxidermist produce a lifelike mount.

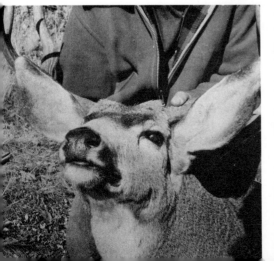

Often, when this happens, a hunter hacks out the horns, and any attempt he might make to save the scalp is inadequate. I knew generally how to peel a deer or elk, but I realized there were many fine points I didn't know. That was why I readily agreed to have Jim show me the proper way to prepare a scalp and that small portion of the skull needed for a good mount.

A few days later I downed my mule buck on the mountainside with a hit behind the shoulders. Jim stood over it, fingering one of the big tines of the rack.

"This is a fine one to practice that caping job on," he mused.

"It's for real, too," I said, "because this is a trophy I'd like to hang on my den wall."

In spite of the early morning chill, Jim took off his heavy hunting coat, laid his rifle across it, and rolled back the cuffs of his hunting shirt.

"The first thing I'd like for my hunters to do," he said, "is take photographs of several features around the head. These should include close-ups of eyes, ears and nose; set of antlers on the skull; and several profile shots to show the relation of each of those features to the others. Pictures made soon after an animal is killed are lifelike. They'll not only help the hunter remember his hunt, but if the taxidermist has those study photographs, he can duplicate the head exactly as it was in real life."

I made the photographs he suggested. Then I took the series of pictures showing how a cape should be skinned out properly, while he explained each step.

I've seen animals caped out, and I've done that job a few times myself. I thought I was pretty good, until I watched Jim. He started by placing his knife point below the withers, at a spot in line with the front shoulder where the leg extended at right angles from the body.

"If you mount a big buck in an alert position," he said, "you need almost a half mount. Many of the scalps that come into our shop have plenty of cape on the withers, but are too short in the brisket. Now watch this."

He cut from the back straight down to the middle of the front shoulder, and across it in a direct line to a point about six inches below the brisket, in a line between the forelegs.

"Most people," he explained, "have read so much about taking out the windpipe to keep an animal from spoiling that when field-dressing or gutting they hack right on up to the brisket part of the scalp until they can reach in and pull out the windpipe. That cutting isn't necessary. If it's late in the evening, or for any other reason you only want to gut the animal, make your opening up the belly to a point eight inches back from the point of the brisket, then cut across like a big T to the middle of the inside of each foreleg and around to the front of each leg. Then skin this flap, or brisket part of the cape, forward about half way up the neck. This lets you take out practically all the windpipe without damage to the cape."

The first cut is straight down the front shoulder to the lowest point on the brisket—and then completely around the animal.

Here the dotted lines show the correct cuts to make when caping antlered game in preparation for mounting.

Next, cut up the back of the neck to a point midway between the antlers.

Carefully peel the hide off the shoulders and the neck.

 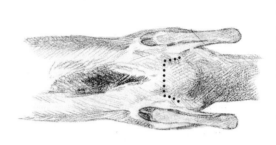

The knife point in the photo indicates the area beyond which the cape should not be split. The dotted line in the drawing shows that the cut should be about six inches back from the point of the brisket on deer, also true for sheep. For elk and moose, however, you'll need more shoulder so that the antlers clear the trophy room wall.

Skin the hide back to the throat, exposing the brisket. Then saw through the brisket so that you can reach in and cut out the entire length of windpipe, which would otherwise spoil quickly.

Make a T-cut across the top of the head between each antler base. Then, to remove the cape, cut through the esophagus to the atlas joint (first vertebra). Bend the head back and cut around both sides of the neck. A simple twist should then separate the skull-in cape from the neck.

But since it wasn't late and we were in no hurry, Jim made his cut completely around the animal. Next he split the scalp from the withers up the back of the neck to a point on top of the head, midway between the antler bases. He peeled the hide off the shoulders and both sides of the neck, then skinned it off the brisket to the very throat of the animal. With this portion of the cape out of the way, he sawed through the exposed brisket, opening it so that he could reach in and cut out the entire length of windpipe.

"For skinning out heads with antlers well apart, like those of a deer or elk," he said, "I make a T-cut across the top of the head between the two antler burrs. For animals with the horn base crowded close together, as in mountain sheep, I don't split the cape all the way to the top of the head. Instead, I make a Y-cut, beginning two or three inches below the top of the scalp and angling a split to the base of each horn."

At this point, Jim cut off the head through the large neck joint immediately behind the skull. He cut right through the center of the "Adam's apple" or esophagus to the bone, bent the head back until the atlas joint (first vertibra) was exposed, then made a cut on each side and on the back, gave a little twist and separated the head from the body. With the head in his hands, Jim could turn it and work on it without having to move the entire deer.

His next step was to separate all skin neatly from around the burr of each antler. On an elk or antelope, this must be cut loose with a knife. Oddly enough, on a deer, the hide is easily pried free with some blunt tool, such as a screwdriver.

Between the antler base and nose lies the trickiest part of scalp removal. You must be careful with ears, eyes, tear ducts, mouth, nose and lips, if you want a perfect cape. I watched Jim cut through the ear cartilage about a half-inch below the outside opening of the ear. Working forward, he stuck his forefinger under the eyelid and stretched it forward. This showed him exactly where the eyelid tissue joined the skull, and he was able to sever the skin behind his fingertip and keep from cutting into or through any portion of the lid.

Immediately below the eye, the tear duct is prominent, and—instead of whacking this off—Jim skinned beneath it, close to the bone, leaving the skin of the shallow duct whole.

At the corner of the mouth, Jim again used his finger trick, cutting just inside the tip of his finger and getting approximately 3/4-inch of inside skin around the lips. He cut off the nose clean, again with the 3/4-inch margin inside the nostril skin.

Jim pointed out that there was no need to burden ourselves on the way to camp with the weight of the whole skull. So he sawed off the skull plate, beginning below the top of the eye sockets and sawing through the middle of the ear butt. From this skull plate he cleaned brains and all excess meat, and this made a flat base that could be fitted on the taxidermist's prefabricated head form during the final stages of mounting back at the shop. The

A blunt tool such as the screwdriver in the left photo, works better than a knife for prying the hide free from a deer's antler burrs. But for elk or antelope, you'll need a knife. Then, as in the right photo, carefully cut through the ear cartilage about a half-inch below the outside opening of the ear.

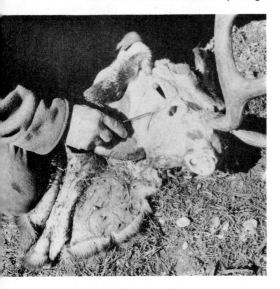

By stretching the eyelid skin forward, you'll be able to see exactly where the tissue joins the skull. Cut beneath the tear duct, in front of the eye.

Also stretch the skin away from the lips and nasal openings so that your cut takes about three-fourths of an inch of inside flesh with the skin. The close-up photo shows one side of the lip already split for salting to prevent spoilage.

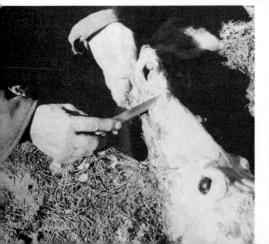 

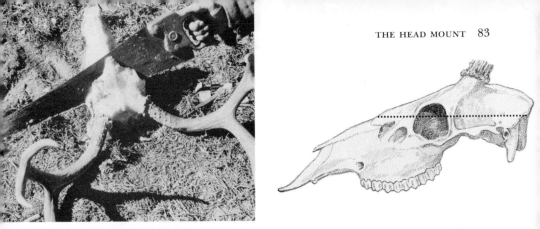

To remove the skull plate, saw across the nose, then just below the top of the eye socket and through the middle of the ear butts.

Next clean all excess brains and meat from inside the skull plate. Thus prepared, the flat-based skull plate is about ready for the taxidermist.

Back in camp, you'll have time to turn the ear inside-out over a short stick and then carefully re-move the cartilage.

lower portions of the skull, such as jaws and teeth, are not needed for mounting and may be discarded.

I asked what kind of knife and saw Jim would recommend for any hunter who might attempt to practice the fine art of taking a cape.

"Any regular hunting knife will do for skinning," he said. "Personally I like a small blade, 3½ or 4 inches long. For cutting bone we use the short, compact, nine-point carpenter saw that is easy to carry. There is also one folding knife available with a blade on one end and a saw on the other. It's one of the finest field-dressing tools I've seen."

In camp, Jim finished the job of preserving the cape. He put the scalp through its final stages by turning each ear inside out like a glove, carefully skinning it loose from the cartilage. To help him in this job, he stuck into each ear a short stick, about the diameter of a broom handle and rounded on one end. He pulled the skin down over this and peeled it away from the cartilage as far as it would go without cutting through where the edges join. Peeling back the ear permits you to salt the flesh side and lets it dry. This keeps the hair from slipping, especially in warm weather.

I learned that the fleshy portions of the lip are also split open, so that salt will soak into them and prevent souring. Any spoiled meat usually results in a hair-slipped spot on the cape.

After all chunks of fat and meat are taken off the skin, the final job is to spread the scalp out in a shady place where the sun won't shine on it at any time and cover it with a layer of salt about ¼-inch deep. No wrinkles should be left unsalted. Rub the salt in well at the base of the ears and around the eyes, nose and lips. A granulated salt is recommended. The guide pointed out that the cost is very nominal even for 100 pounds and is well worth packing in to your hunting camp. If you don't have salt, stretch out the cape as the old trappers did with their beaver pelts, and air-dry it as quickly as possible in the shade.

Spread out the salted cape for at least 24 hours to drain and dry some. Then shake off the wet salt. Then resalt, but not so heavily this time. Roll up the cape with the salt inside, and pack it for the trip to the taxidermist. If the cape is to be shipped, Jim recommends packing in a plastic garbage can or plastic lined bag to keep the salt-drawn juices from leaking all over. He warns against any wire, colored string or other object which might stain the hair.

"All this," I said, "is well and good. Now all we need is a top taxidermist to help us put it together again."

Since he himself fits that category, Jim grinned. Then he was serious again.

"You really should choose your taxidermist before you go hunting, to know you've got a good one who will make your mounts lifelike and natural. And a pro is always better than the back-room hobbiest and moonlighter."

Taxidermists don't just "stuff" animals anymore. The word "taxi" means arrange or move about; "dermis" means skin. Together they indicate moving or arranging the skin.

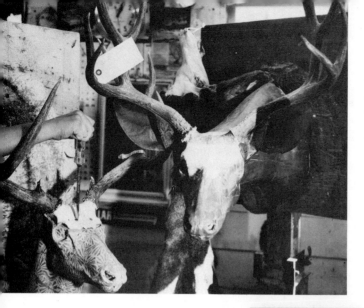

Here a taxidermist screws the skull plate into a block of wood set in a standard pressed-paper form. The makings of the author's own mount, at the photo's right, already has the ear liners in place.

The taxidermist sets false eyes in water clay and follows with detail work around the eyes and nose. He then fits the cape over the form. After the mount has dried, the taxidermist applies paint and then a finishing coat of varnish to simulate moist areas around the nose and eyes.

This is the author's finished mount as it now looks on his den wall.

The re-creation of an animal, Jim explained, means that a clay reproduction is modeled, or sculptured in the position desired and then cast. In the negative mold, a form is made of pressed paper, though sometimes other material is used. The antlers or horns on the skull plate are fastened securely to a block of wood in the head of the form.

The glass eyes are set in water clay. Detailed modeling around the eyes and nose is also done in water clay, which incidentally, is the same as potter's clay. The clay is simply mud, like the kind that can be dug out of river banks, except that water clay can be fired or baked to make pottery.

The tanned, prepared cape is then cemented over the form. When the cape is dry, the color of the bare skin on the nose and lips and around the eyes is restored. Then a touch of varnish to the areas that were moist on the live animal finishes the trophy.

According to Jim, a good taxidermist must be an artist as well. I agree.

Methods for caping out a scalp and handling the horns of sheep, antelope, moose and such are approximately the same as that Jim Gay showed me for deer. Naturally more effort and time are involved for the larger animals. It's not a bad idea to learn to do this job yourself so that you can check to see that it is done properly. You don't always have a guide capable of properly cutting, fleshing and handling the skin for a top-class mount, and there may be times when you are alone and have no help of any kind.

To cape a wild boar or javelina, you make the first cut in a similar pattern around the shoulders to the one described for deer. Normally, however, you don't have to cut up the back of the neck since the neck is large enough so that the skin can be cased—that is, peeled off over the head of the animal, as one would "peel" instead of pull a glove off his hand.

After the skin is stripped to the ears, those cuts around the ears, eyes and nose must have the same careful attention required for scalping any other big-game animal. This takes time but is worth it for a trophy mount.

BEWARE OF KICKBACKS

On that first trip I made with Jim Gay, he confided a bit of information that made me think even further about having first-rate trophies. He knew that I had hunted in most of the far corners of the continent and over the years had collected a sizable number of fair trophies. What Jim told me in our Platte Ridge camp, he later put together as an article for *Outdoor Life* magazine, and from a couple of experiences I'd had, I knew it made a lot of sense.

Jim said that while the vast majority of guides and taxidermists were completely honest, there were among both professions certain individuals who traded business back and forth at expense to the hunter, both in money and in shoddy work.

Jim told me that this racket worked two ways. In one the taxidermist—often a fellow who does such a poor job that he can't get enough work to keep him going—approaches the outfitters or guides with the proposition that if they send heads, hides, horns to him, he will kick back a certain percentage of the fee paid by the hunter for taxidermy work. This means, of course, that the taxidermist adds the kickback fee to the hunter's bill. And the head or other mount often suffers from a quick and poorly done job.

Jim didn't have to convince me because I'd had that experience. Once on a western hunt I took a much better than average sheep head. I should have been suspicious when the outfitter recommended an eastern taxidermist when he was surrounded by some of the best-known names in the business. But since he assured me that the eastern concern did the best job on sheep of anyone he knew, I allowed myself to be suckered in.

When the mounted head came out of its shipping crate, the first thing I noticed was that the neck looked more like that of a giraffe than a wild sheep, and the second was that my bill for the job came to a much higher figure than that advertised by some of the reputable firms where I'd had work done in the past.

But when I put the long-necked sheep on the wall, I thought no more about it until about a year later when I moved my animal to another location in the den. When I took it down, I shook a handful of hair and a double handful of bugs out of it. The thing was literally crawling with weevils. I took it carefully outside and soaked it with bug spray. When that dried, I soaked the mount again until I was sure I'd destroyed every critter between the hair and papier-mache form.

I brushed out another handful of hair before I put my sheep back on the wall. It looked reasonably good if a guest didn't inspect the lips where some of the hair was missing, and the base of the horns, where the receding scalp line showed about half an inch of skull. I thought a number of times I'd send that moth-eaten head to some reputable taxidermist such as Jim Gay or Joe Jonas, but have kept it to remind me how much of a sucker I had been not to make my own arrangements with people I know who have good reputations.

On the other side of the coin, as Jim Gay put it, there are guides and outfitters who approach taxidermists with the proposal that the taxidermist will get a kickback for all hunters recommended by the man who deals in heads and hides. The guides who have to follow such a procedure are usually second-rate, with few repeat customers. Again the hunter is cheated, both by a poor hunt and by the kickback tacked onto his bill in one way or another, usually as a hidden charge.

"I have known instances," Jim said, "when the guide and taxidermist got together. Both got kickbacks, and the poor hunter had to pay both charges without knowing it."

I asked my outdoor partner what an ignorant hunter such as I could do about this, though I thought I knew the answer.

"As for the taxidermist," he said, "check him out in advance. If possible, see some of his work. Ask for references. He doesn't mind giving them if he is capable and honest. If you are satisfied with him, let him give you shipping tags and instructions. Then send the instructions on trophy preparation and shipping to your outfitter or guide, though an experienced outfitter is already acquainted with all those details."

As to the selection of an outfitter, it's all right to take the recommendation of a reliable taxidermist, for men in the business can tell much about a guide by looking at the heads, capes and skins he send in. But go a step further. Check with the game department of the state or territory where you plan to hunt. They generally know a great deal about the guides there and can help you contact previous clients of some of the guides.

Many years ago I made my first hunt to the Yukon Territory in northwest Canada. I knew no one there or any person who had hunted there. Though my method took time, here is how I went about selecting my outfitter for one of the finest big-game hunts I ever had:

I wrote to the Game Department at Whitehorse and asked for a list of guides in the Yukon. With this list in front of me, I studied a map of the territory and selected three of the outfitters who appeared to be the farthest removed from the towns and highways. I wrote identical letters to each of these three, asking about his hunting territory, method of transportation, length of hunt, guides and prices. The most straightforward and intelligent answer was from a fellow who told me all I had asked but said he thought he had a "full complement of hunters," though he was still waiting to hear from one of them. I liked the way the fellow wrote and knew I would like him as well. After another exchange of correspondence, the outfitter finally did have a vacancy, and I was in.

7

Mainly Bears
and Cats

THE BEAR HAS long been one of the most sought trophies on the continent. From the usually mild-mannered black to the cantankerous grizzly, man has held a vast respect for members of the bruin clan. Going after bear has been considered one of the big hunting adventures. More dramatic stories have been told about the acquisition of a bear rug than perhaps any other kind of trophy. Many guides and other wilderness men with whom I have talked have had hair-raising experiences with bears. And often these men had scars to prove what they said.

Even to those most familiar with the shaggy tribe, bear country is always a fascinating place. Here there is continually an element of suspense and danger, for although most bruins simply vanish at the first sight or scent of man, a backwoods traveler never knows when he will suddenly come upwind on a mother bear with cubs or an ill-tempered old boar with a toothache or a deep hatred based on some past experience for anything that smells like a human. Impressive is the fact that the more a woodsman knows about bears, the more he respects them. I've hunted with several guides in the far corners of isolation who did as much hunting behind themselves as they did ahead. Since we were in big-bear country, I did not have to ask the reason why.

Some of my most vivid memories of explosive action stem from the bear rugs I have on my own den floor and from those in the trophy rooms of friends. A special story goes with each one, and woe to a new friend or acquaintance who doesn't know any better than to ask where and how I bagged any certain one of those bears. The old friends have long since learned enough to keep the subject to more trivial things.

All but one of those rugs came from bear in prime condition and had excellent taxidermy work on them. That's about all a hunter can ask of any trophy.

To accomplish his part of the job, a hunter has two things to think about before he sends the hide to the taxidermist. One is the condition of the fur

A comparison of one of this brown bear's deadly meat hooks with the hand of guide Paul Springfield makes it apparent why some guides in bear territory spend as much time looking behind as ahead.

before he pulls the trigger, and the other is the proper handling of the skin in the field. Often the latter chore is up to the guide, but every hunter should know enough about skinning to see that his guide does a good job.

Many times the shooter must skin out a bear on his own. This is what happened to me on an Alaska marsh, and the guide was there with me.

We had toppled a big brownie at the edge of a salmon stream. The time was late afternoon. After we made sure the old boy was dead, we stood over him for a few minutes admiring the long-haired pelt. Then the guide said, "Well, he'll be all right here tonight. We'll come back in the morning and skin him."

"What's the matter with now?" I asked.

"To do it right," he admitted, "I've got to go look at the book."

"You build a fire," I said. "I'll take the hide off this critter."

I guess I didn't do the job as well as an expert would have, but I gave the guide a lesson in skinning a bear, explaining the steps as I went. As it turned out, I was glad to have the guide along. He proved to be pretty good as a pack horse and I let him manhandle the heavy hide to camp.

The first step in taking a rug your friends will admire is to get a good pelt, and that's not always easy. The best two seasons are in fall, just before bears go into hibernation, and in spring, shortly after they come out of their dens. Over many years the general game seasons in the far northern part of the continent ran through August or a part of that month. I've seen some patched and ragged coats come out of those regions. To be reasonably sure of a full-furred pelt, you should hunt in the spring in that portion of North America where bears hibernate and during the winter months in more southerly latitudes where the black bears are usually up and active the year round.

Of course a fellow doesn't always have time enough to study the best fur coat in the vicinity and make a choice. I was on my haunches in an Alaska alder thicket when a tremendous brownie passed along one of the trails at close range. It was August and he was near enough so that I could see where he had rubbed off patches of fur, and new hair was filling in those spots. He was upwind of me, but he stopped and stood for long minutes as though he suspected my presence. Maybe a vagrant breeze had carried a wisp of human scent to him. I didn't want to shoot him, and those close quarters plus his ragged hide gave me a double excuse. I was relieved when he moved on. If he'd come at me, I'd have had no choice.

One late fall, a half century ago in Montana, I was almost naive enough to try something foolhardy. I was young, vigorous and certainly brainless enough to have tackled Hell with a bucket of water.

It was late in the fall with a smidgen of snow on the ground and very cold. My ranger friend had found a bear den that showed all signs that the bear had gone into hibernation. Scattered fragments of bear grass, which is often used to make a bed, led into the cave. There were no tracks to indicate that the bruin had left its hole for some time. We stood before the hole, and the ranger drew his six-inch blade out of the sheath.

"You'd like to have a trophy you'll remember," he said, "so I want you to take this knife, crawl in there and kill him."

"I never realized," I said, "how stupid I must look."

"I'm not kiddin'," he insisted. "A bear in hibernation has a slow pulse beat and is in a state of stupor. Jab the knife in at the base of his throat and you'll sever his jugular. When he bleeds to death, we'll drag him out."

"Okay!" I agreed, brashly. "Gimme the knife."

To this day I have no idea whether I'd have crawled into that cave. Nor do I know if he'd have let me. I guess he wanted to see how far I would go before he stopped me. The bear itself saved me any embarrassment and no doubt did the ranger out of a good story, when it suddenly popped out of the hole, took a quick look at us and galloped into the timber as if someone had shoved a cocklebur under its tail. The critter sure didn't look to me as though it was in any stupor. I handed the ranger's knife back.

"Maybe he'll sleep more soundly tomorrow," I said.

I have no idea how many bears I've watched at their various activities of berry picking, digging for rodents, fishing, making their marks on trees, or just ambling along in no hurry and, seemingly, with no destination. Away back yonder when I killed my first bears, a bear was a bear was a bear. And I gave no thought to size or condition of hide. To my mind, I was a mighty hunter who had taken life and limb in hand and downed ferocious, charging creatures—only two of them had been standing still and the others had been charging in the wrong direction. Not until later years did I begin to carefully look over an animal for size and condition of pelt before I decided to try for it. I've passed up many more than I ever shot at.

I can assure you of one thing—a bear always looks twice as big when he's on all fours and four times as large on two feet than when you've finally put him on the ground. Unless you're a most competent woodsman yourself, you should have a guide to help you judge size and also help determine the condition of the skin. My taxidermist friend Jim Gay tells me that sometimes tanning will tighten up loose hair, but there is no guarantee.

Now you have your mount or trophy rug down. It's big, with long, rich fur and you can visualize it in your den or trophy room. It's too heavy to hand-haul back to camp. No horse will pack it, for the smell of a bear terrifies most horses, and before a horse will take a hide, you have to rub a handful of bear fat around his nostrils to overpower his sense of smell.

You've got to take that hide off the carcass. The simplest way is to let the guide do it. If you know how to help, you can make a much quicker job. In the field you don't have to do the fine work on the hide or skull. That can come later in camp.

THE SKINNING

Jim Gay says that even before you begin to skin, certain measurements should be made for your taxidermist to help him re-create the animal as you first saw it. Many big-game hunters and guides carry steel measuring tapes as a part of their gear, and all should. Those measurements the taxidermist is interested in are length of the body from the nose around the curve of the back to the tail; length of the head from the base of the skull to the top of the nose; circumference of the neck; circumference of the forearm; circumference of the chest behind the forelegs; circumference of the belly; and length of tail. Regardless of what you think you have seen, bears do have tails. The tail vertebra of a black runs about five inches long, and a grizzly's is about half as long. Along with the measurements, a few close-up pictures might also be of help.

For a head mount you must still cape out the shoulders and pull the skin back over the skull. But for a rug the field-dressing job is usually quicker and simpler than the job you will have when you get your hide to camp, especially if you take the head off the carcass at the base of the skull and plan to skin it later.

The field skinning steps are simple. Most experts I've watched make a cut from the vent down the back of each leg to the center pad of the paw. Then they cut from the vent to the tip of the tail and then up the center of the belly and chest to a point where the cut can turn at right angles to a corner of the mouth. Cuts are then made from the chest down the inside of each foreleg to the pad.

On the back legs, Jim tells me that some guides start their cuts about six inches up the belly from the vent and from there down the inside of the leg to the pad. This, he says, leaves enough hide at the back of the pelt to give the finished rugs a more square appearance.

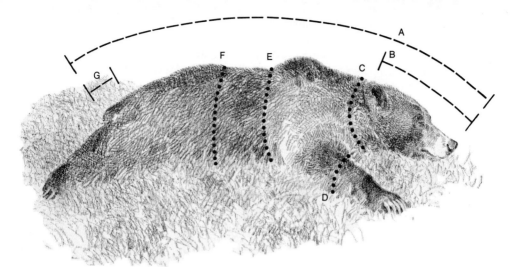

Before turning a downed bear for skinning, record the following measurements for your taxidermist: **(A)** length from nose to tail, **(B)** length of head from nose to base of skull, **(C)** circumference of neck, **(D)** circumference of forearm, **(E)** circumference of chest, **(F)** circumference at belly, **(G)** length of tail. Then take close-up photos.

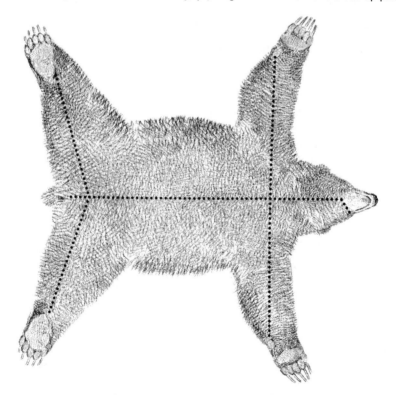

These are the basic cuts for a rug. The back leg cut, started six inches up the belly from the vent, leaves enough hide to give the rug a squarer appearance than results when the cut is begun at the vent—a common practice.

When you make those cuts, your job of getting the hide off is by no means finished. It doesn't strip off as easily as that of a deer. In most places it's a matter of pull-hide-and-cut, separating the skin from the meat and being careful not to slice through the hide. Do not leave chunks of fat on the skin. It's not, however, necessary to do too close a job on the fat. That can be a chore for camp.

Now, Jim advises, if you want a life-size mount, go one step further in the field. Measure the carcass, making approximately the same measurements that you made before you started skinning. This gives the taxidermist a better chance to acquire the right size mannequin for a lifelike mount.

Back in camp, the tedious part of this hide preparation begins. Detailed attention will pay off in a handsome trophy. In skinning out the head, you must give the same care to the ears, eyes, nose and lips as for a deer scalp, or any other. These cuts are made in about the same manner as shown in the deer skinning pictures in the preceding chapter.

The ears should be turned inside out, "like turning the fingers of a glove," as Gay puts it. Leave one inch of skin inside the lips. This should be split open from the flesh side so that it lies flat and can be saturated with salt. Skin the feet to the toenails and leave these claws attached.

Stretch the green hide over a log or tack it, flesh out, against a wall. Then cut off all fat and meat left from the field skinning. This is an easy chore, but it takes time.

Then stretch the hide flat (if not already tacked up) and measure it from the tip of the nose to the tail and across the width between the tips of the two front paws. Added together and divided by 2, this gives what is called the "square" of a hide. A green hide has a lot of elasticity. When tacking it on a wall, a lot of guys have a tendency to pull it as long and wide as possible to get a higher "square" score. This stretching of the pores often loosens the hair, which may or may not be tightened in the tanning process. Don't take a chance on pulling the skin any more than medium tight. It will shrink back to a bit less than natural size in the tanning process anyway.

Salting is the next step. Jim Gay suggests, "salt the hide well, using fine granulated salt, applied in a layer about ¼-inch thick. Pay special attention to the tight places such as the paws, ears, eyes, tail, and the split skin of the lips. After salting, leave the bear skin spread flat, out of the sun, for about 48 hours if possible. Then shake off the wet salt and re-salt the hide.

If you are able to ship the salted hide immediately to your taxidermist, roll it up and place it in a plastic garbage can. These cans make the best shipping containers, provided they are not too roughly handled in cold weather, since cold plastic is brittle.

"Metal garbage cans are satisfactory only if they are completely lined with good heavy plastic, or if the bear hide is almost dry. The hide may be put in a burlap bag and then in the can if there is any chance that the juices will run out. Many galvanized cans react to the salty brine which exudes from the bear hide in such a way as to dissolve the hair. Sometimes the galvanizing may be defective, or the can may have been used several times so that the galvanizing is depleted. Then rust stains may form during shipment."

If you cannot ship the hide immediately, then tack the salted hide, flesh out, to a wall until it is dry and can be shipped. The dry hide may be rolled loosely and sewed in burlap for transportation by express.

If you think you have a record bear, then you should by all means preserve the skull. The recommended way to do this is to boil the skull in soapy water until you can remove all meat. Then bleach the skull and coat it with plastic to help prevent cracking of the teeth. Be sure to save any teeth that loosen or come out. They can be glued back.

RECORD SKULLS

Since hides are so elastic, the Boone and Crockett Club, which maintains records on all North American big-game animals, bases its record measurements of such animals as bears, cougars, and jaguars on skull measurements, taking the length and width of the cleaned skull sixty days after the kill. Since the average shrinkage of the skull over a two month period runs only in sixteenths of an inch, the green skull will give a reasonable indication of whether it will make the record books.

The records of bear skulls in the Boone and Crockett Club's *North American Big Game* (1973 printing) show that the largest Alaska brown bear ever taken had a skull length of $17^{15}/_{16}$ inches (without the lower jaw) and a

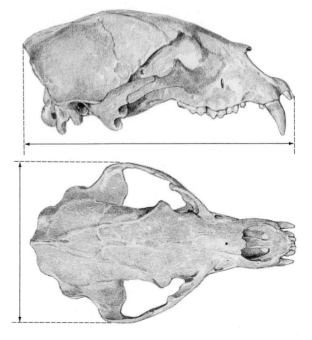

The Boone and Crockett Club recognizes only two measurements for bears and cats. These are greatest length along the long axis of the skull, without the lower jaw, and greatest width. Malformations are excluded. Official measurements are made with calipers to the nearest sixteenth of an inch. The skull shown is that of a black bear.

width of $12^{13}/_{16}$ inches for an added total score of $30^{12}/_{16}$. The smallest brownie skull that made the records book measured 18 by 10, for a score of 28. Anything between the two might get your name into the book.

The largest black bear was $13^{11}/_{16}$ by $8^{11}/_{16}$ inches, for a score of $22^6/_{16}$. The smallest in the records measured $12^{11}/_{16}$ by $8^5/_{16}$, for a score of 21.

The grizzly records show a top skull of $17^6/_{16}$ by $9^{12}/_{16}$ for a $27^2/_{16}$ total, and then range downward to $14^{11}/_{16}$ by $9^5/_{16}$, for a minimum qualifying score of 24.

The top polar bear—no longer legal game—was $18^8/_{16}$ by $11^7/_{16}$, for a total of $29^{15}/_{16}$. The smallest measured $16^{14}/_{16}$ by $10^2/_{16}$, for a 27 score.

All of this might give you an idea of how your skull measurements might stack up with the largest bears taken in "fair chase" over the years.

THE SHRINKING SKIN DILEMMA

Jim Gay tells me that possibly the most vociferous complaints that any taxidermist endures are those centered around the size of the bear skin a hunter thinks he sent in and the size of the final rug returned to him.

"Some guys," he said, "get right mean about it. They accuse the guide, outfitter and taxidermist of keeping their big bear skin and substituting one half the size, or of getting the hides mixed up and sending one that belongs to somebody else."

I can understand this. Many years ago when I got my first bear rug, lifted it out of the shipping crate and spread it on the floor, it looked like a coon hide compared to the size of the one on the bruin I thought I'd seen rearing up on its hind legs in an effort to identify a movement I'd made.

Before I blew my stack over the rug, however, I made some measurements—a job I should have done on the green hide before it went ot the taxidermist. Lying flat on the floor, it didn't look like much. But then I determined that a measurement of more than 7½ feet across the skin from the tip of one front paw to another meant that such a bear would have stood at least three-feet tall at the shoulder. The measurement of more than eight feet from the tip of the nose to the hind foot would have allowed the animal to loom up on its hind legs as tall as I remembered. With this realization, I was awed all over again and completely satisfied that this was the rug I'd collected.

There is some shrinkage in the tanning, but usually the tanned hide is about the same size as the green hide laid out flat before being stretched.

You can be assured that your guide or outfitter is just as anxious for you to have your own trophy as you are. When the hide arrives at your taxidermist's shop, it is immediately punch-labeled with the number of your record card. To be doubly sure, many taxidermists also punch in your initials.

OTHER NORTH AMERICAN GAME

Such animals as the cougar, jaguar, wolf and coyote are skinned out in much the same manner as a bear, with the same cuts and a similar treatment of skin and skull. The cougar and jaguar are the only cats listed in the Boone and Crockett Club records. The minimum qualifying score for the cougar is a length-and-width skull measurement totaling 15 points. The minimum for the jaguar is 14⁹/₁₆.

Over many years the wolf has been a prized trophy but is not considered in Boone and Crockett Club records. I have a wolf rug taken from the far northern Yukon years ago, when the animals were plentiful and considered unwanted predators. Now, however, with the wolf on the very brink of extinction, I would certainly never add another to my trophy list.

FOREIGN TROPHIES

Since many hunters go to Africa and other places outside this country to add to their trophy collection, a word here on care of trophies in the tropics might be in order. For such advice, who else should we turn to but Jim Gay, whose experience with skins from the four corners of the earth led him to the preparation of a bit of advice to those who would ship in their capes, skins and other trophies from foreign places.

To comply with U.S. Government regulations, alien hides must be dipped in a solution approved by the U.S. Department of Agriculture. The dipping rids the hides both bugs and germs. Then the hides must undergo other specified procedures.

Recommended are two formulas for dipping. Each is stirred and thoroughly dissolved in 50 gallons of water. One formula consists of 50 pounds of salt with 20 grams of sodium fluoride. The other includes 50 pounds of salt and 10 pounds of sodium arsenite. Both are successful, not only in purifying the hide but also in providing a certain amount of temporary tannage which keeps the hairs from slipping.

Ordinary hides are soaked from 24 to 48 hours, depending on the size of the skin, and stirred every four hours to give good penetration.

According to regulations, the hide must be thoroughly dried before shipping and there must be no tainted or moist flesh attached to it.

To help clear customs and other inspection, the trophy must bear a certificate showing that it was taken from an area free of hoof and mouth disease and that it was properly dipped.

Wart hog trophies are shipped separately, for they must be dipped again when they arrive in this country. And the shipping containers are burned.

Jim Gay says that you are more likely to get your trophies home in good condition if you have your own shipping crates made where you hunt, usually where the outfitter has his starting or ending station. Most good outfitters have a carpenter who does this. The crates should be lined with waterproof paper. But it's always wise to check the regulations beforehand with officials of the U.S. Department of Agriculture.

TROPHY CARE AT HOME

One thing I've noticed over many years is that the average fellow seems to know little about taking care of trophies *after* he gets them into his home. I own a few old, worn-out, beat-up skins I thought were indestructible.

One of my prize rugs is from a cougar taken out of the rugged Gila wilderness in New Mexico. For years I kept it on the wall in my bedroom where it remained in immaculate condition. Then we moved. I had no space on the wall at the new place and deposited the rug on the family room floor where anyone going through the room would cross one corner of it. Soon the thin skin on one side was broken and a portion of it was worn.

I have one Alaska brownie that I treasure because he and I came to reasonably close quarters before the fates decreed that he should go down first. I value the rug more than my treatment of it would indicate. That rug has really been "lived up." Had the rug been on its feet instead of on the felt, I'm sure it would have so resented my abuse that it long ago would have tried to crawl out of my den and escape.

When I brought the brownie home, our house had a leaky basement. I had my work room and some of my trophies in these lower quarters, but most of the trophies were on the walls. We did everything we could to stop that basement from flooding but nothing seemed to work. When it rained, it poured—in. And it always seemed to rain hardest when we were out of town. We'd come home and find the old rug swimming around in about a foot of water. After we'd pump out the place, we'd hang the rug on the line in the back yard to dry.

In addition to this water treatment, the brownie rug got walked on and stumbled over. Every kid in the neighborhood made a game of trying to pull off his ears or yank his hair out. He was abused, but he'd been put together by a first rate taxidermist and stood the test of time.

He's in a place of honor now. His flanks are thin. He is ragged in spots. Most of his claws are gone. But to me he remains a lovely mount and almost everyone who sees him thinks so.

The best place for trophies is a trophy room—if you can afford one—or on den walls. Or if your rugs are on the floor, they should be in one of the less traveled rooms. Though trophy rugs are called "rugs," they won't last very long where traffic is heavy.

If a man who knows his business has converted that skin into a rug for you, after you've done the preparatory work, and if you take care of the finished product, you'll have a lovely and valued trophy that will endure until your grandchildren get old enough to look upon it as evidence of those tall tales they'll hear you tell.

8

Small Game

WITH A GREAT VARIETY of available game the early Americans probably didn't depend solely on a diet of squirrels. But the bushytails did contribute a sizable share of meat to the vigorous appetites of our pioneers and backwoodsmen.

It has been said that the development of the Kentucky long rifle, the most accurate gun until then, revolved more or less around the need to assure a family of meat on the table. And tree squirrels furnished their share of sustenance to the sharp-eyed woodsmen.

Since a direct hit from a large caliber rifle of this period would tear a squirrel apart and leave only fragments of meat, squirrel hunters learned to "bark" a squirrel, leaving the body intact. This was done by shooting the heavy lead ball just far enough under the animal so that the explosion of bark either killed or stunned it long enough to be otherwise dispatched. From the moment he was old enough to lift both ends of a rifle at the same time, a youngster did his share to keep the family fed. Usually his first game came from the squirrel clan.

Today, wild meat is not the important factor that it once was, but most of the modern rural and suburban boys start their hunting by going after squirrels. Squirrels were my first game, and it was always a proud day when I could bring home a "mess" of bushytails. My weapon was a single shot .22, and I've never used any larger caliber for either gray or fox squirrels. I credit this little game animal with whatever woodsmanship I may have developed in my younger days.

Squirrel hunting is by no means confined to beginners. I've met some 80-odd-year-old youngsters in mountain squirrel woods and in my favorite swamps. You'll find them anywhere from nine to ninety with the same keen eye and bubbling enthusiasm. Some of the states list squirrels as their Number 1 or Number 2 game animal and the treetop dweller is always high up in the list of popular game, especially in most states east of the Continental Divide. He's a favorite, too, in many of the western mountain states, and there he may come in other species.

For one-cut squirrel skinning, cut across the lower back, as shown above, and then insert a couple of fingers under each side of the slit. With one swift motion, you can rip the hide from stem to stern. Platters full of squirrel, as in the photo at right, help account for the fact that the little critter is the Number 1 game animal in some parts of the country.

The choice of guns for squirrel hunting ranges anywhere from the .22 to a 12-gauge shotgun with No. 6 shot. I've always preferred the .22, with the long rifle cartridge, said by some experts to be the most accurate bullet known. I use a 4X scope and shoot for the head. If I hit, the animal dies instantly, and a miss is almost always a clean one. Long ago I learned that a body shot often leaves the animal with enough stamina to crawl into a tree cavity and die a painful and possibly lingering death.

According to the most technical of the textbooks, a couple of dozen species of squirrels are found on this continent—and any number of subspecies. But I was never mammalogist enough to recognize more than a few, such as the gray, fox, red, Abert and Kaibab—all of which I have encountered hither and yon. I always thought the latter two much too pretty to shoot, even when I was out after squirrels. Most of my hunting has been for the gray and fox squirrels, abundant in the eastern states.

In my early teens, I frequented the river swamps on my weekends and cooked for lunch whatever game I happened to have taken. When I had squirrel, I skinned out each one as carefully as if it were a valuable silver fox. Then I put the carcass on a spit to roast over my campfire. Once when I was occupied with the skinning, an old swamper came up and after greetings, squatted on his heels to watch.

"You sure go about it the hard way," he commented.

I handed my second squirrel to him. He picked up the skin on the back with one hand, cut through it with his knife, making the slit wide enough to get a couple of fingers under the hide that peeled toward the head and two more fingers under that part toward the tail. With one slick-as-you-please motion that took about two seconds, he peeled that bushytail from stem to stern. I'd been working on the first squirrel about five minutes. That swamper's method is the one used by most squirrel hunters I know, and became the one I used thereafter. I am certain there must be many ways to "de-hide" one of the tree-toppers.

The next neatest and quickest method I've seen was employed by a mountaineer who cut through the hide around the squirrel's tail, slit the skin along both legs, far enough to give him a grip, held the squirrel's tail under his foot on a log and ripped off the fur in one swift movement.

Of course in both instances he had to peel the hide from both hind and fore legs to the feet and cut the feet off. I also cut off the head rather than skin it out until my old mountain friend George Shuler took me to task.

"Bring the heads to me," he said. "They're the best eatin' part of the critter. Them brains is good."

"I usually bust them up pretty well with a .22 bullet," I pointed out.

"Saves me from having t' crack 'em," he said.

Since that time I've tried squirrel heads, and while they're not much to look at, they do make good eating.

As with all game animals and birds, the more quickly you cool out your meat, the sweeter it will be. Some states have hot weather squirrel seasons. But animals bagged during high temperatures and piled in the sun are more likely to spoil than those treated more moderately. Whatever the weather, some hunters I know field-dress each squirrel as quickly as it is killed by ripping it open and taking out the guts. If they intend to remain in the same spot and continue hunting, they will often cut through the skin of a hind leg, expose the tendon and hang their kill on a twig. If they are moving from place to place, some gunners will string their squirrels on a cord tied around the waist to let the animals get plenty of air. One hunter I know uses a mesh game bag. Another carries small, plastic bags; after his squirrels have cooled out, he dresses each and drops it into a separate bit of plastic. All of these methods beat piling the animals in a hunting coat pocket or tight game bag as soon as they are killed, and leaving them there perhaps for hours before giving them proper care.

If you want to save the hide for a mount, you must go about the skinning much as I did before the old swamper gave me that demonstration. Most taxidermists, however, prefer to skin the animal themselves. For years I kept two mounted squirrels, one on each side of the mantel above my fireplace. One was a fox squirrel, taken at the mouth of the Suwannee River, the lowest spot in eastern North America, and the other a "boomer" or red squirrel that came from the top of Mt. Mitchell in North Carolina, the highest spot.

I skinned out each of these by cutting around the vent, an inch or two along the tailbone on the underside, until I could get a grip on the bone and pull it out of the tail. Then I cut along the inside of each leg until I had enough space to cut the legs off and pull them out to the feet, much the same as stripping a finger out of a glove. From that point on, it was easy to peel the hide down around the carcass to the front legs, again stripping them out, then over the head, taking care around the ears, eyes and nose. The "cased" skin was stretched over a V-pointed board before being salted and allowed to dry. Then it was tanned and made into a mount.

For eating, I usually cut each of my squirrels into six pieces — four legs, rib case, and loin — unless I plan to run them through with a spit and broil them immediately over a campfire. The best way to preserve the pieces for future use is to pack them in a carton, covering them to the top with water, and quick-freezing. Protected by the water, the meat will keep in the deep freezer a long time and won't be freezer-burned.

I have one friend who won't eat squirrels because she claims they look too much like rats. But take it from a lot of us, any of the larger squirrels that has fattened on a diet of nuts, seeds, fruits or the kernels from some farmer's corn field makes one of the tastiest dishes you ever flipped a gum over. Eat him fried, broiled, barbecued or hacked up in a stew, and you'll be obliged to agree with me.

RABBIT

My early boyhood memories include lying awake with my window open on a cold winter night and listening to Gene Lee's beagles, down the road a way, set up a ruckus at whatever beagles set up ruckuses at. I often wondered whether it might be a coon or cat or some wandering spirit of the night, or whether the pack was holding choir practice for the coming Saturday. The music never failed to send a shiver of anticipation through me, for ever since my arms had been strong enough to hold a gun and my legs long enough to keep up, I had taken a part in those hunts that started at daylight on Saturday morning and usually lasted until dark.

Mr. Gene, more than three times my age, was a lean, wiry man who knew more about rabbits and hunting them with beagles than anyone I ever met. As long as I knew him, he kept a pack of two dozen or more of the little hounds. And when they spread out along the rim of a swamp, they could make the timber ring with melody. We never had less than a dozen hunters on those Saturday forays. Sometimes we had twice that number, and every one as enthusiastic a hunter as Mr. Gene himself.

We'd hunt the hillsides along the swamp for cottontails and get into the swamp for the long-legged "cane cutters," or swamp rabbits, that could run like a fox and swim like a muskrat and gave us some of our most exciting races. I'm sure the beagles enjoyed them as much as we did.

Such days do not, by any means, belong to the past. Though such hunting stems from colonial days, there are more beagles and more rabbit hunters today than ever before. In some parts of the country the rabbit is now classified as a game animal where often in earlier years he was considered a mere nuisance that preyed on gardens and other crops. Or else he was so far back in the wilds that no one ever bothered going after him. Some of the southern states now declare the cottontail as their Number 1 game species, based on the number of hunters and man days spent in pursuit.

There is more than one occasion on which the rabbit would have had my vote as Number 1. Once at noon in the wild Savannah River swamps on the Georgia-South Carolina line, a companion and I discovered we had left our lunch in the car, miles away. The day was Thanksgiving and we were expecting a big feed that evening, but here we were, with breakfast at least eight hours behind us and dinner almost that many ahead. The only game we'd seen that morning was a swamp rabbit I'd jumped out of a cane patch and now had swinging on my belt.

While my partner built a fire, I stripped the hide off our rabbit, dressed it, flavored it with a small vial of salt I always carried in my kit, and ran it through with a hickory spit. We enjoyed that Thanksgiving feast there in the heart of the river swamp, down to gnawing the bones. My buddy later declared that it was even more tasty than the turkey he had with all the trimmings later in the day. I agreed, but we didn't tell our "wimmenfolks" so.

Back in my days with Gene Lee, I learned early to field-dress a rabbit as soon as I had killed it. I didn't get those guts out because I wanted to cool the carcass, but simply to eliminate some of the weight. When we hunted, we covered a lot of territory. And often, getting to where we knew a rabbit would circle back to its starting point was a matter of running, so weight was important. On these occasions I might have had anywhere from four to eight rabbits slung on a belt around my waist. They weighed less minus the insides.

As I picked up each bunny I'd bagged, I cut around the vent to release its hold on the intestines. Then I held the rabbit by the upper part of its body and slung out the insides with a quick whipping motion. That was in the days before I knew that the liver and heart were delectable.

At least half a century passed, after those first rabbit hunts with Mr. Gene, before I learned that using my knife to empty those rabbits of their insides was a waste of time and that if a man only knew how, he could do a much cleaner job than with a knife. This information came from my friend Charlie Marshall, the same fellow who taught me to skin a deer with a golf ball. Charlie says he learned about rabbit gutting from John Henry, an old Negro woodsman friend who lived on the edge of Cooleewahee Creek swamp in southwest Georgia. Charlie hunted many a day with his old friend, who told him how he had "discovered" this knifeless method of dressing. Here is the story Charlie Marshall told me about John Henry and his rabbits:

"John Henry hadn't always stripped his rabbits as he killed them. In fact, he had never given it a thought until (his wife) Mattie told him the meat tasted better if the rabbits were dressed immediately after being shot. This stands to reason, because the shot makes small passageways which provide avenues for the intestinal contents to seep through and ruin the best part of the rabbit, the loins. Following Mattie's advice, all rabbits John Henry killed were cleaned immediately by conventional methods; that is, he opened the rabbit with a knife and pulled the intestines out by hand. It was a cold, messy job when the temperature hovered around freezing. But it was worth the effort, since rabbits made up a good portion of the family diet during the middle thirties.

"One rainy November afternoon, however, he forgot his knife and had no way to open the rabbit. Being a man of few actions, and a little on the lazy side, he surely didn't want to walk all the way back to the house to get a knife. That was when he stumbled on the knifeless operation."

Marshall explained how he did it:

"He would grasp the limp body behind the front legs with his right hand and squeeze hard. The left hand was then placed below the right, and it too was used to compress all the insides toward the rear of the rabbit. At this point the hind part of the abdomen was twice normal size.

"Now John Henry prepared for action. He spread his legs about eighteen inches apart and flexed his knees. He lifted the rabbit above his head while compressing with both hands. Then as if he were calling on magic powers, he would sling the rabbit toward the ground, striking his forearms against his knees while holding the rabbit very tightly in his big, rough hands. When John Henry straightened up (Would you believe it?) there on the ground behind him lay all the insides of the rabbit. The quick stop caused intestines, heart, liver and lungs to be expelled through a tear near the anal opening.

"With very little practice, you too can gut your rabbit with one quick motion. The cavity will remain clean because it has not been opened and exposed to hair of other rabbits or bits of trash in your game bag. Rabbits cleaned in this manner will cool much faster, and are not nearly as heavy to carry during the remainder of the hunt.

"It should be pointed out that with a very large rabbit, a small cut in the skin between the legs will make the job a lot easier."

As Marshall pointed out with John Henry, the rabbit has always been a large factor in the home economy of the south. Back in those days before the government handout programs, many a rural family lived largely on their garden plot and what wild meat they could get out of the woods—a good percentage of it cottontails and swamp or marsh rabbits. Many fami-

This knifeless method of field-dressing a rabbit starts the desired cooling of the meat with no mess and little time lost. The procedures include squeezing the innards toward the rear until they bulge the area to twice its normal size and then slinging down hard, striking your forearms against your thighs, and letting the momentum thereby expel the innards through a tear at the vent.

lies I knew preferred rabbits over the chickens they raised in their back yards.

At my house we cut rabbits up much the same way as we prepared our squirrels—in six pieces.We always found that if we refrigerated the meat for several days before cooking—which was less time than for processing larger game—the cooked meat was more tender. I thought then, and still think, that refrigeration also helps the flavor. We prepared rabbits in a number of ways. Two of my favorites were broiling them and frying pieces that had been rolled in dry flour. My mother had another recipe, too, that was hard to top. As one of my hunting companions put it, "If you'll bring Mrs. Elliott a rabbit, she'll use it to make up the best batch of chicken salad you ever ate."

Along with a few million other Americans, I am a dedicated rabbit hunter. Those late fall and winter days of rabbit hunting are hard to top with almost any other type of upland game hunting: The air is cold enough to gel, and the music of a beagle rings like a bell.

For rabbit, there are a few things I do a little differently now. I use a lighter shotgun, with No. 6 shot. I don't run quite as fast to get in front of a circling bunny. I don't try to carry as many cottontails or swampers hanging around my belt. And when I field-dress a rabbit by slinging out those insides, I have along a plastic bag to save the heart and liver, which are mighty fine eating.

I had to agree with one of my old outdoor partners—almost as ancient as I—that "there just ain't any country people anymore." What he meant, of course, was that with all modern conveniences available to almost everybody, one phase of our American culture is passing out of existence. The vast majority of our citizens no longer have to grow what they eat or get it out of the woods. But there may come a day, sooner than we think, when we have to get back to basics if we want to survive. Heaven help us if any invading army ever decides to bomb all of our supermarkets out of existence.

Throughout the woods of North America a number of the smaller fur-bearing animals served as food for our early settlers, and to some extent as clothing. Chief among these—after the squirrel and rabbit—were the beaver, muskrat, raccoon and opossum; the first two vegetarians, the raccoon partly so, and the possum more omnivorous than the others.

MUSKRAT AND BEAVER

As a lad, I made at least a part of my spending money from muskrat hides. Every morning through the winter I was on that trapline by daylight and usually just made it to school under the wire by the time the bell rang. I wasn't so much as a trapper, but I caught enough of the animals to give me visions of developing into a modern John Jacob Astor.

I cased out the muskrat hides, stretched them on shingles and showed them to my buddies to prove that one day I would be a wealthy fur trader.

Muskrat, opossum, raccoon and beaver are all edible fur bearers. But some meat hunters pass up muskrat and beaver because of the "rodent look."

Word got around, and one of my teachers asked what I did with the carcasses. When I reported that I buried them, he looked aghast, then said, "You are missing some mighty fine vittles. How about bringing those rats to me after you skin them."

I kept him supplied with one or two at a time for the balance of the trapping season, always with the thought that there must be something a little odd about a fellow who apparently enjoyed the carcass of a rat. And I didn't find out why he liked muskrat until years later when I paid a fancy price for a gourmet's dinner where the main entree was marsh rabbit, which I learned was the fancy name for muskrats out of the Maryland marshes.

I've never tried beaver but understand it carries a chunk of palatable meat, and that it contributed substantially to the diet of the early western mountain man.

Muskrats and beavers are fur bearers and nowhere can we find them classified as game animals. Few "sportsmen" will go hunting for one or the other, but one gunner I know makes a game animal out of the muskrat. He owns a couple of fish ponds with earthen dams. When the muskrats begin digging holes in them, he sits on the hillside early and late and picks them off with his varmint rifle. He makes his kills on dry land or around the edges, so that he can retrieve the animals.

"It's better than varmint shooting," he claims, "and it sure makes for some fine eating."

CASING FURS

The muskrat continues to figure rather prominently in the fur picture of the United States, and buyers of these raw furs want them "cased." To prepare fur in this manner, cut around the vent and tail, and out the back side of the legs to the feet, which you then cut off. Then pull the hide over the body to the nose, with the front feet off, and stretch it on a frame or board cut to a V at one end so that it fits into the narrow part of the skin around the head. Stretch the skin flesh side out, and remove fat and meat before allowing the hide to dry.

The casing method is often applied to other small fur animals such as the fox, mink, fisher, skunk and opossum when they are caught for fur. For rug mounts, Jim Gay tells me that most taxidermists prefer a lynx, bobcat or raccoon skinned flat, as described earlier for the bear.

The beaver, for its fur, is handled a bit differently in that you cut it from tail to chin, and peel the legs out without splitting to the feet. The skin is then stretched on an oval frame and sewed to the sides of the frame in such a manner that the skin itself retains its oval shape. The early mountain men started this flat processing of beaver skins so they could store and transport them in compact units. They usually did the job with slender green poles bent into a circle and tied. With the skin held in place, the pole circle could be expanded to stretch the hide.

RACCOON AND OPOSSUM

Two animals that fit the category of both fur bearers and game species are the raccoon and opossum, both favorites of American hunters since the days of the coonskin cap. Except for some of the deserts and highest western mountains, the raccoon occurs just about universally where there are trees. And the possum inhabits many of the northern and midwestern states, as well as the South and the far West Coast.

The coon hunters are a clan unto themselves. They develop and train dogs to hunt nothing but old ringtail. They buy and sell and trade these hounds, sometimes by freight all the way across the country and trust one another implicitly when it comes to prices, payments and the return of animals if a buyer is dissatisfied. They love the deep woods, the dark of the night and the ringing chorus of their hounds along a ridgetop or in the heart of a swamp.

Most state game authorities where the raccoon is found will tell you that the coon population there is higher than it has ever been. In spite of that, in many places the old dyed-in-the-ringtail coon hunter is passing on. With the tremendous explosion of the deer population, the younger hunters are devoting themselves to the larger animal. Thus the raccoon does not have as many disciples as once it did. But a persistent breed holds on.

There has been another change too. A large prime coon hide once brought a fancy price. (Remember the days of the coon-skin coat?) Many a farm boy had his traps strung out along the creek for the old granddaddy coon in the vicinity. There is still some traffic in hides, but not at the level of a few decades ago. Now, even as then, many woodsmen hunt coons for their meat only.

Some years ago, I belonged to an organization called the Pheasant Pluckers Association. Twist those syllables around any way you want, and they add up to a hilarious occasion every time we met. One reason for our existence was to get together once a year over a feast of game meat, with our members furnishing the game out of their freezers. We employed the best chef in the city. Since our Pheasant Pluckers Association was made up of small and big game hunters, the table offered every kind of wild meat from bullfrog legs to buffalo steaks. No one had the capacity to partake all of the many dozens of varieties.

One year we came up with every kind of local meat but a raccoon. I was elected to fill that order. I knew a friend with coon hounds, and he agreed to take on the job with me. The story of our wild night in the woods is too long to tell here, but the chef knew his business and there wasn't a scrap of coon meat left. I still have that coon hide on my trophy room floor, right in the middle of the five bear rugs from all over North America. My visitors examine that coon with something of wonder. When they ask what in the world it's doing there, they never have to twist my arm to get the story.

There are many reasons why the opossum has always been one of my favorite characters. One is that we grew up together. From the time I was old enough to climb a tree, I knew every possum den within three or four miles of my house, and I paid them regular visits in late fall and winter. The animals seemed to prefer those shallow hollows where they could curl up out of the wind, and peep over the edge if they heard any noise worth investigating. Every hollow of this type always yielded a few possums each season.

In spite of the price lists put out by a number of raw fur traders, the hides didn't bring much. So I built up my own local trade with some of the old-timers who considered possum meat choice eating. And of course I always kept enough for our family needs.

An opossum generally lives on fruits, berries and such, but is not always too particular about its diet. So the trick was to keep one in a pen for two or three weeks and fatten it on table scraps, sweet potatoes, apple cores and such until we decided it had eaten itself "clean."

The accepted way of preparing possum for the table was much like that we used to dress a hog. We had water boiling in the old iron wash pot and to this added a cup or two of lye water. We broke the animal's neck by holding its head against the ground with a stick under our feet and pulling on the tail. We dipped the carcass in the boiling water until the hair was loose, then scraped the carcass clean. I've heard somewhere that the musk glands under the forelegs should be removed before dipping, but we never did and it didn't seem to affect the taste of the meat one way or another.

We gutted the possum. Then we cleaned and usually parboiled it slowly until it was tender. Then we baked it in a pan with red sweet potatoes or yams. A few people I have known wouldn't eat the meat because they thought it was too greasy, but the way we prepared it at home, it never turned out that way.

It was customary to parboil a possum carcass to remove fur, but after one experience I've always wondered whether it was necessary. One of the best portions of possum I ever ate came my way the night I spent with a mountain family in the southern Blue Ridge Mountains. After dark, we turned the dogs out and went off into the hills on a hunt. I remember scaling cliffs, wading icy streams and falling out of a tree. We were back home at midnight with three large possums. We skinned them out, tacked the hides on the barn door, and put our possums in the pot, with a hatful of sweet potatoes. I don't know who kept the fire going the remainder of the night because I was sacked out in a feather bed that simply gulped me into its maw the moment I lay down. Next morning, however, I was up in time to see the animals quartered and fried and was ready when the parts were served with slabs of sweet potatoes and coffee that was black, hot and thick enough to float a mule shoe.

That kind of breakfast is sure designed to sober a fellow up.

9

Game Birds

ONE INTERESTING STATISTIC would be the number of shotgun shells exploded each year at feathered game. It is true that most of the states make hunter surveys which help them in estimating the amount of game taken during the seasons, but there is hardly any way of accounting for those flying shot strings which fan empty air. Regardless of the misses, the amount of feathered game killed in the United States each year runs into astronomical figures. Almost all of it is used as food, but now and then some prize specimen or unusual skin shows up, and the gunner decides to preserve it.

Amazingly enough, few shotgunners know how to take care of their game birds in the field. And later they don't know to preserve birds as top quality food or save the skin for a trophy. Over the years I've seen many game birds spoiled simply because they did not receive the proper attention, and these included almost every species from doves to the magnificent wild turkey.

As with game animals, large and small, one of the most important first considerations is cooling out a bird carcass as quickly as possible after it has been shot. The air temperature can be a big help in preserving game, as well as a factor in spoiling it. But regardless of the weather, not many hunters take the time or trouble to insure getting sweet, fresh meat for the table. During the hunt, the action may be so fast or the excitement so intense that the only thought is the moment.

FIELD CARE OF UPLAND BIRDS

The early cooling process may depend both on the field conditions and the size of the bird. During the early dove season, for instance, which exists in some parts of the country, temperatures range from warm to hot. I shudder when I blink the sweat out of my eyes and see some guy in the adjoining stand pile his doves on the hot ground to soak up the hot sun. I stifle an

111

Here Canadian geese take flight. To ensure proper cooling of the meat, the author cleans large birds immediately in the field. He sometimes places smaller birds into a cooler, guts and all, and tackles the cleaning job at home.

impulse to walk over and tell him that he's mistreating a fine game bird and explain how he should spread out his doves in a shady spot on the ground and keep an occasional eye on them to be sure they are not covered by blowflies or ants. If there is a lull in the action, he might even take time to pinch out the crops which lie at the base of the neck and which over a period of time in hot weather can result in spoiled breast meat. Even in cold weather, the freshly killed doves should not be piled together, but spread singly on the ground. They cool out more quickly that way.

Naturally, birds such as quail, woodcock, the rails, prairie chickens and others, which are not hunted on stands, must be handled a bit differently in the early stages. As these are bagged, they must be carried, and in most instances they are carried in the rear game bag of a hunting coat. The season for such game is usually later in the year and the shooting is slow enough so that the birds have a chance to cool out in the game pocket before more birds are piled on top. Some fellows I know carry birds in ventilated pockets or bags. Many who hunt quail by vehicle or wagon leave their birds in it as they are killed.

One fellow I know, who hunts afoot, pinches the crop out of each bird as his pointer brings it in. He finds this easier to do after first slitting the skin around the crop.

"Removing the crop serves two purposes," he explained to me. "One is that it helps protect the meat in hot weather, and the other is that I can study the contents of several crops and learn generally where the birds are feeding. If several of them have soy beans, then I'll spend some time hunting the edges of the soy bean fields. The same goes for corn left by a mechanical harvester, or for beggarweed. Finding forest weed seeds makes me take to the woods."

If I plan to be away for two or three days, I haul along an ice chest and refrigerate my birds. If they don't get too hot just after they are bagged, a refrigerator will keep them, guts and all, until I get home to clean them properly. If I plan to be away longer, I usually dress out my birds and either ice them down or quick-freeze them and bring them home wrapped with a chunk of dry ice.

Once I got smart and had the cook in the hotel where I was staying dress a limit of quail and hold them for me in the kitchen refrigerator. When I got ready to leave, he smilingly handed me my neatly wrapped package. I paid him for the job and tipped him liberally. When I arrived home after a drive of 300 miles, I unwrapped the parcel to repack my birds for the deep freezer. You've already guessed it. I brought back exactly half the number of quail I'd left with the cook.

FIELD CARE OF LARGE BIRDS AND WATERFOWL

Large birds such as wild turkeys and some of the waterfowl are cooled out more quickly by field-dressing them immediately after they are killed. This is especially true when the weather is warm or even mild. Under these circumstances, I go so far as to draw the insides from my grouse, pheasants, geese and most of the ducks. The same procedure is used for all. Pluck the feathers from around the anus to expose the skin for an inch or more on all sides. Slit the skin all the way around the vent until the end of the intestines can be pulled out a short distance. Then widen the opening in the thin skin along the bottom of the belly. The intestines slide out like a long rope.

This is as far as some of the hunters go until they arrive back in camp or at home. I go further. With the opening at the lower part of the abdominal cavity large enough to put my hand in, I pull out the remainder of the insides — heart, liver, lungs and as much of the windpipe as I can reach. Then I wipe out the cavity with a handful of moss, ferns or a clean cloth. With a gobbler, I tie a stout cord around its neck, hang it up to drain while I smoke a pipeful of tobacco. I place the liver (minus its gallbladder), gizzard and heart in a plastic bag. I bring the bird out with its head over my shoulder, and the drainage is usually completed on the tail of my hunting coat or the backs of my hunting pants legs. With a wild gobbler over his back, who cares?

One of my woodsman friends claims that when he is in camp where no refrigeration is available, he dresses out every game bird, large or small, in the manner I described for turkeys, then sprinkles the insides with a liberal dose of salt and pepper before hanging the birds up to drain. The smaller birds, he ties on a cord, separated enough so they do not touch. Then he ties the cord between two trees, high enough and in such a way that the birds cannot be reached by stray dogs or varmints.

As I write this, I have before me a news release put out by a fellow who has a reputation as a conservationist as well as a hunter. He writes that "the flavor of doves is considerably improved if the breasts are pulled out in the field and kept in a chest or insulated bag filled with ice." I'm sure he did not mean that only the breast of a dove is worth saving. It is true that this small triangular piece of meat is the tastiest and most flavorful known, but eating the breast only and discarding the rest is a sacrilege. Every scrap of meat on the carcass of a dove is well worth the effort needed to gnaw it off the bones. One fellow of my acquaintance, with a large mouth, good teeth and a cast-iron stomach, doesn't even waste the bones. He simply bites off half a dove at a time and chews up the whole thing. He really shows an appreciation for the little creatures.

Except when I plan to be away for any extended period, I always wait until I am home to complete the dressing of my game birds. In this final processing, a good many people I know take the easiest way out and skin their game, especially the smaller varieties as quail and woodcock. To me, skinning any game bird is almost in the same category as peeling the breasts off a dove and throwing the rest away. Would you buy a chicken at the market if it had been skinned?

REMOVING THE FEATHERS

Much of the fat and flavor of any bird lies just under the skin, and when it is cooked, this outer covering helps to hold in the juices and keep the meat tender and moist. While I must admit that a skinned quail is better than no quail at all—and I've eaten many bobs and hens with the hide peeled off— there is a definite difference between a plucked and a peeled bird.

For some of the largest upland game birds such as blue grouse, ringnecks and turkeys, I am not averse to dipping them in boiling water to help take the feathers off, just as my grandmother used to do with her Sunday dominecker chicken or Thanksgiving turkey. You don't leave them in long enough to cook the skin but only long enough to loosen the feather bases so that they turn loose easily. Most of the time, more than one dipping is necessary to remove the heavier feathers.

To thoroughly clean a bird, sometimes it is necessary to pull out the very new or "pin" feathers. And where some bird has a layer of "fuzz" feathers or down left form the original picking, these may be burned off by passing the bird back and forth over a flame. My grandmother used the log fire that heated her house; my mother, a blazing sheet of newspaper.

Dressing waterfowl is a ball game all its own. Did you ever try to dry-pick a duck or goose? This is a good way to get your mind off any other worries you might have. Dry-picking has been done down through the ages, of course, with the result of at least one valuable by-product. The pioneer folk picked their ducks and geese in two layers. They first removed the outer covering of stiff "contour" feathers. Underneath was the dense coat of soft new feathers, generally known as "eider down," a term probably brought over from middle Europe where the eider duck was common and was stripped for its heavy undergarment of feathers. The down that was plucked separately from the coarser or stiffer feathers was packed in bags and saved until there was enough for a pillow, quilt or a mattress. Back in the mountains, when spending the night with highland friends, I've slept on down mattresses a few times. Usually these mattresses were thin and spread over another mattress of shucks or other harder material, without which they would possibly have engulfed and digested me.

In this more modern age, we are blessed with such things as sleeping bags and clothing made out of "prime northern goose down," but it's possible that much of this contains some duck down, which is just as effective at holding body heat in and the cold out. Now that we can buy our comfort in garments such as these and other modern conveniences and no longer have to depend on our ingenuity and patience to produce them by tedious effort, we take the quickest possible way to get the feathers off our waterfowl.

The method I recommend as the most practical for removing feathers is to have it done by a commercial firm that specializes in dressing poultry for the market. Usually, too, in regions where duck hunting is heavy, you may almost always find people who open a shop in season to dress out all ducks and geese brought in by hunters. I have always found the charge for this to be nominal and certainly well worth it for the time I saved.

There are times, however, when you must dress out your own waterfowl, and there's no way other than to roll up your sleeves and get at it. The easiest technique I know employs paraffin wax, usually used for sealing jelly glasses. We buy our paraffin wax in quarter-pound packages from one of the major oil companies, but many drug and variety stores carry it. A couple of these packages will easily handle from three to six ducks, depending on the size. We drop the blocks of paraffin into a bucket or pot containing 2½ to 3 gallons of water and bring it to a boil. When the wax melts, hold the duck by its feet, dip it in and stir it around for a few seconds. Hold it over the pot and let it drain. Then lay it out on a newspaper, preferably in a cool spot to let the wax harden that has soaked into the feathers. If I have so many ducks that they absorb a lot of paraffin and thus thin out the mixture, I toss another chunk or two into the pot. The stuff doesn't cost more than a few cents a block.

Don't be in too big a hurry to finish this job. Let that paraffin get as hard on the duck as it was in the package. This creates a sort of shell that penetrates through the feathers to the skin. You can peel this off with your fingers as easy as peeling an orange. You may have to try this with ducks on two or three occasions before you learn how much water and wax you need for the various kinds of birds, how long to keep each submerged, and exactly how to swish the bird around to get maximum penetration of paraffin. But when you become proficient, you'll agree that this method is one of the easiest for undressing waterfowl. One of my friends claims that he has also tried paraffin-dipping on some of the smaller upland game birds and that it works well, except that with a thin-skinned bird you must be careful not to peel off the skin with the coat of feathers.

AGING THE MEAT

You may hear many notions on what to do with your game bird from the time you bag it until it's on the table as the main entree. One of the theories I've heard a few times is that you should gut a goose or duck and then leave it hung by its tail feathers until the body weight pulls the bird loose before you finish dressing it. This is supposed to properly "cure" the meat. The only experience I've had with this method occurred when two ducks cured in this manner were presented to us by a hunter friend. Well, they didn't smell to suit me, and I wouldn't have passed them on to the dog. I later learned that this was the way the guy treated all of his waterfowl and was a little sorry that I hadn't given them a try, even if it ended in ptomaine. I must admit that I like my meat a bit fresher.

I think it improves any meat—including game bird—to cure it for a few days at temperatures slightly less than 40 degrees, and I do this by storing it in a spare refrigerator we keep for such purposes. Smaller game goes through the same curing processes as heavier red meat, but doesn't take as long. I'll store quail three or four days before eating or freezing them. I kept an old gobbler at this temperature for as long as eight days and found him mighty tender. I keep constant check on any meat curing in this manner, to be sure that it doesn't spoil.

PRESERVING THE MEAT

The final chore in dressing a bird for the table or freezer depends to some extent on how you plan to cook it. Normally a larger bird such as turkey, goose, duck or pheasant—to be roasted whole or baked—is cleaned out well inside with the carcass left whole, just as you usually buy domestic fowl. This rule, however, like most general rules, has its exceptions. I know one backwoods family that cuts up every critter they kill into pieces small enough to fry in a skillet. The reason is a practical one. They have no refrigeration other than cold weather and the spring house, so when there's a surfeit on meat, the simplest way to keep it is to cook it, pack it in jars, top-off the jars with lard, cap them tightly and store them in the cool root cellar.

Just as with domestic fowl, the liver, gizzard and heart are choice tidbits. Some prepare them as a part of the main dish and others use the giblets in gravy. One game bird prized for its very large gizzard is the coot. It lives on aquatic vegetation and apparently grinds a lot of this through its enlarged organ. Most of the gunners for this rather unusual bird also consider the breast as good fare, and I have found all coot meat most palatable.

I'm sure you will agree that freezing is the easiest and best way to preserve your surplus game birds taken in a short season but hopefully held for enjoyable repasts later in the year. Rural electrification being what it is, there are few families now, unless they are in the far backwoods, who do not own some type of artificial refrigeration.

When we are lucky enough to accumulate a small surplus of such game birds as quail, doves, woodcock, snipe, rail, chukars and you-name-it, we dress them and cure them for a few days before packing them tightly in plastic cartons of several sizes. One small carton may hold two birds— enough meal for our family. Another carton may hold six, which we use when we have guests. We fill each carton with water and tape down the lid with plastic tape. Then with an indelible pen, we write on the carton the date and the kind and number of birds.

Every game bird is best frozen in water, though we don't always do this. Freezing in water helps to retain freshness and moisture over long periods. It's not necessary to encase the meat in ice if you plan to use it within a few weeks or months. The freezing dries the meat and can leave it a lot like cardboard if it is left there long enough. For meat that you wish to wrap only and not freeze in ice, a special freezer paper is available almost anywhere. This helps to hold the meat in good condition. Amazingly enough, we kept a wild gobbler tightly wrapped in this freezer paper and frozen for almost two years. I was expecting the cooked bird to come out with about the same taste and tenderness as a white oak knot, but it was delicious.

THE TROPHY

A game bird is usually kept as a trophy for one or more of three reasons: its beauty; its unusual coloration, or the story behind it. Rarely is a game bird preserved for its size alone, as are mammals or fish. There are exceptions, of course. At his Ichauway Plantation in southern Georgia, my friend, Mr. Robert W. Woodruff, has the mount of the largest wild turkey ever taken on the plantation. As a trophy, this is a beautiful bird. It has additional value because it was bagged by Grantland Rice, generally conceded to be the most famous sportswriter of his generation.

I've kept mounted bird specimens around me ever since I can remember. The earliest were results of my own feeble efforts at taxidermy, but each had its special significance either for its unusual coloration or for the memories it called forth. Since I could never afford to keep my mounts under glass, one by one they wore out from the handling of well-meaning friends who would stroke the birds or pull on their feathers in order to get a better look at them. The only fully mounted bird specimen I have at present is a huge colorful cock pheasant that reminds me of some unforgettable days with Gabby Barrus, a special hunting partner in Wyoming. I keep that trophy in a secluded nook and watch my visitors rather closely to see that the bird does not get pulled at too much.

Some of the professional taxidermists tell me that most of the birds they mount display an unusual color phase. Albino or partial albino is the most common, but once in a great while a bird may be in the melanistic or black phase.

I get calls from people who tell me that they have bagged something such as an albino teal with only the blue showing it its wings, or a black-headed quail, or their first grouse, and most of them want to know, "How can I go about getting this mounted?"

TROPHY DEEP-FREEZE PRELIMINARIES

I always tell them the easiest way is the best — to have the job done by a competent taxidermist. If the bird is freshly killed, there are certain steps the hunter should take. If the feathers show blood, they should be sponged off gently with warm water and a soft cloth, rubbing in the direction the feathers lie. Blood that dries in place, hardens and mats the feathers. Blood creates problems for the taxidermist and often leaves a stain. After they have been washed, the feathers should be allowed to dry.

Most taxidermists would like to have the bird frozen before delivery to the shop. Taxidermists are usually behind in their orders and will themselves have to freeze the bird until they can get to it. You don't have to be an expert to freeze a bird properly. After cleaning and drying the feathers where necessary, lay the bird on its back with wings folded as neatly in place as possible. You can carefully "comb" the feathers in place with the back of a small knife blade or some similar pointed instrument. The bird should then be wrapped in smooth paper or plastic and laid in the deep freezer where it will not be disturbed until you are ready to take it to the taxidermist.

A few times in my peregrinations around the top side of this old globe, I have had a bird whose skin was unusual or valuable to me in one way or another. And I had no way to freeze the trophy or to preserve it other than by skinning. I was fortunate in that I'd done some work on study skins and in taxidermy too under the direction of Dr. Thomas D. Burleigh, who many think has contributed more to ornithological research and knowledge than any man since Audubon. His two books, *Birds of Georgia* and *Birds of Idaho,* are classics.

SKINNING FOR A MOUNT

Taking the hide and all its feathers off a bird of any size is not as simple as skinning a rabbit or squirrel. Some birds are easier to peel than others, for they have tougher hides. Most of the ducks, for example, are not as fragile as birds such as the woodcock, which Frank Woolner, one of my outdoor partners and an authority on the subject, says "has a skin like wet toilet paper." A dove sometimes sheds its feathers at the slightest touch.

If you can't freeze the bird or preserve it another way, you should know the essentials for taking the skin off. You'll need a sharp knife and a cupful of dry meal. The meal will absorb blood you might start with your blade.

1. Place the bird on its back and flatten or spread the wings to get the wing feathers out of the way, as illustrated on the next two pages.

2. With your fingers, push back the feathers in a straight line between the anal opening and the lower end of the breast bone. Then slit the skin along this line without penetrating the abdominal cavity.

3. With your fingers and fingernails and some help from your blade where necessary, peel back the skin from the abdominal wall and around the thigh until the thigh is exposed enough so that the upper portion of the leg may be severed from the lower. Leave the lower leg in place.

4. Work the leg carefully out of its covering of skin to the upper end of the tarsus, or knee joint. Cut and strip all flesh off, leaving the upper leg bone intact. Treat both legs in this manner.

5. With a good grip on the base of the tail, bend the tail up and cut through the tail muscles and backbone immediately behind the vent, being careful not to cut through the skin or the butts of the tail feathers.

6. From this point, work the entire skin back over the body of the bird, pushing the wings forward to loosen any stiffness there. Work the skin around each wing bone where the bone joins the body. And when the bone is exposed, cut it loose from the body.

7. Continue to work the skin over the neck and over the skull to the beak. With some birds, the head is too large to pass through the skin of the neck. So you have to make an incision along the neck skin. The taxidermist can sew this in the final mounting job, so that it doesn't show.

8. As with all mounts, be careful about cutting around the eyes and ears. On small birds this job may be particularly painstaking.

9. When you have worked the skin to the beak, cut off the skull at the back end, close enough so that you can dig out the brains. Cut out the eyes, tongue and all excess meat around the skull. (Leave the skull attached to the skin.)

10. Skin out the wings to the last joint and cut out all remaining flesh.

11. Then salt the skin, returning the contours as nearly as possible to their lifelike condition, as when the body was inside. Arrange as many feathers as you can in their "live" appearance. After a day or two of drying the "skin," wrap it neatly in a plastic bag or in paper. The bird is now ready to be delivered to the taxidermist.

SKINNING FOR A MOUNT

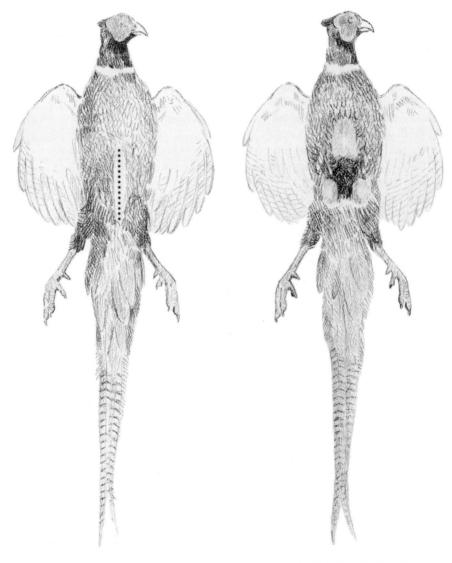

Steps 1 and 2. Spread the feathers between the anal opening and the breast bone. Then cut the skin without penetrating the abdominal wall. (These captions summarize the steps described in the author's text on the preceding page.)

Steps 3 and 4. Peel the skin back from the abdomen and also from both thighs such that you can sever the upper leg from the lower part. This way you leave the lower leg and feet attached to the skin. Then strip off all flesh from the lower leg bones.

Step 9. With the skin peeled to the beak, cut off the skull at the back end and dig out the brains. Then cut out the eyes, tongue and all excess skull meat, leaving skin and skull attached.

Steps 5, 6, 7, 8. Cut through the tail muscles and backbone immediately behind the vent, without cutting through back skin or the butts of the tail feathers. Work the skin over the body and cut each wing bone where it joins the body. On some birds the head may be so large that you'll have to make an incision along the neck skin in order to peel the skin to the beak.

Steps 10 and 11. Skin out the wings to the last joint and cut off all flesh, as you did with the legs. Salt the skin and restore the contours as nearly as possible to their "live" appearance. After a day of drying, the skin can be delivered to the taxidermist.

Parts trophies such as the beard, spurs, and tail are prized among turkey hunters. You can dry the foot with the toes spread so that it will stand on its own by first propping it as shown and then holding the spread foot down with a weight. In removing the tail be careful not to cut through the butts of the tail feathers.

PARTS TROPHIES

Where a hunter does not want to go for the "whole hide" of a game bird, parts of some of the larger birds make striking trophies. The tail, for instance, on a turkey or grouse may be cut and dried in the shape of a fan, just as it appears during the mating ritual. This makes a colorful wall piece.

To remove the tail, you cut it loose near where you would cut when taking the whole skin, except that you must sever it all the way through and separate it from the body and the skin. Again, take care not to cut through the butts of the tail feathers. Thoroughly clean that small portion of back-bone at the base of the tail of all meat, and then salt the area. Spread the tail feathers out like a fan, with the outer tips of the feathers just touching. Then place the fanned tail between boards or stiff cardboards and allow it to dry until it retains its fan shape without collapsing. You can mount the tail on a wall in this manner or have the taxidermist put a fancy base on it.

Prized trophies among wild gobbler hunters are the beard and the spurs. The old toms usually sport long, heavy beards and carry sharp, lethal spurs. The length and sharpness often helps indicate the age. You'll find little more than a nubbin on a year-old bird. The beard and one leg are often tied together and hung up as the token of a hunter's prowess. When it dries thoroughly, the leg should be coated with heavy shellac. This helps retain the skin color and texture. Some hunters I know dry the feet with the toes spread and the leg upright, so that the foot will stand on its own. This is done by spreading the toes when they are pliable, propping the leg up against a support, and holding the spread foot down with a weight.

10

And Fish

No Meat or Trophy preparation book would be complete without a chapter on how to treat a fish. In the first place, fishermen outnumber hunters by several times. With the vast number of fish species, the almost unlimited types of aquatic conditions, and the myriad ways of catching fish, there are few places on the continent without a fair number of anglers. And no matter where fishermen are, from the kid after hornyheads in the creek to the big-game devotee, you'll find almost every one as dedicated to his method as the angler next to him or a world away.

The percentage of fishermen who know the most practical methods of caring for their meat or preparing trophies is probably no larger than that for hunters. I've seen fish handled such that within a few hours they were unfit for human consumption, whereas they would have made delicious eating. Also on record are many stories of game fish which definitely would have gone in the record books had the angler been aware of the importance of his catch.

WORLD RECORD LARGEMOUTH

The world record largemouth black bass was recorded officially only through a lucky series of events. This record has stood for forty years. And even though it set a record, the bass was lost to posterity as a mounted specimen because the fellow that caught it did not know enough at the time to have it mounted. The story is a fitting one here.

When George Perry went fishing on June 2, 1932, he was after meat for his hungry family. He owned an old rod and reel and one underwater plug he had bought with hoarded five cent pieces. Whenever he hooked the plug on a snag too deep to reach with a paddle, George simply pulled off his clothes and dived to retrieve it.

124

George was fishing in Montgomery Lake, an old channel of Georgia's Ocmulgee River, which was sealed off when flood waters made a new channel through the swamp. He had taken a lot of bass out of this lake, but on that early June day, he fished all afternoon without getting a strike. About dusk he was on his way to the boat landing, where he kept his bateau tied to a shoreline tree. He put down his paddle and made one last cast to an old underwater snag near the landing.

This final effort produced his only strike and only fish of the day. It was a monster bass, but George Perry was elated because the fish meant meat on his table for several meals.

On his way home, George stopped at the store in Jacksonville, Georgia, a village near the Ocmulgee River, to buy a loaf of bread. A group of fishermen, lounging in front of the store, asked the universal question: "What'd you catch, George?"

"Aw," he said, "I didn't get but one, but it's a pretty good bass."

"Let's see it."

"I'm in a sort of hurry, but—well, all right."

He showed his fish and was a bit irritated that his friends wanted to weigh it on the store scales. When they didn't believe what the store scales indicated, they delayed Perry even further by walking across the street and weighing the fish on the Post Office scales. One of the fellows had the bright idea of getting an affidavit from the postmaster.

George, thoroughly annoyed by now at being held up, carried his fish home and ate it. His friends sent off the evidence of his record catch. Geogre didn't realize the importance of that last cast of the day or the value of the delay he'd suffered in Jacksonville, until he began to receive mail with congratulations, questions from other anglers, and assorted fishing tackle and equipment from manufacturers.

You can hear many stories similar to this, but few of them have such a happy ending. And some are real tearjerkers that involve all sorts of misfortunes. A catch may not have been verified properly. Or the fisherman may have thought that much larger fish had been caught. Or some guy didn't recognize the species, and simply carried his fish home and ate it—to hell with a record.

Obviously most fish are caught for the purpose of eating. Fish is an important source of protein all over the world. Consumption runs into astronomical figures. Fish meat offers a percentage of minerals, and the sea-run varieties are said to be a source of edible iodine.

AS FOOD

One important discovery in recent years, made by U.S. and by English research teams, working independently, was that fish flesh is not only polyunsaturated, but it helps to dissolve the saturated fats created in the blood by the fat of red meat and many dairy products. Cholesterol is regarded by the medical profession as a blood thickener that collects deposits of fatty tissue along the walls of the veins and arteries, and eventually releases portions of these deposits into the blood stream as clots that can cause blockage of a vein or artery, resulting in a heart attack, or a stroke if one of the clots reaches the brain.

Investigations showed further that people along ocean coastal regions who live mostly on a diet of fish have fewer heart attacks than those in the interior who are red-meat eaters. Fish flesh then, theoretically, might be credited in this regard as contributing to a longer life span.

Naturally you should take proper care with a fish if you want to have quality eating. The degree of caution depends on the fish itself. Unlike red meat, the fresher fish flesh is, the better eating it will be. Some fish spoil more quickly than others. Frank Woolner named the bluefish as one of these.

"A bluefish," he pointed out, "is something like sweet corn. If you stumble on the way back from the corn patch, it's too late! Ideally, a blue should be cooked while it is still in rigor mortis. I say *before they quit wiggling*. For prime table use, a bluefish is bled immediately after capture, gilled, gutted and placed on ice. The things are prone to go soft in a hurry, even more rapidly than sea trout.

"Striped bass are much harder fleshed, but should be kept cool. Ideally, gill, gut and place them on ice. If no ice is available, use a burlap bag well-wetted with sea water. Evaporation will keep them cool. They keep well, even in the round."

Mullet is another "soft" fish, in much the same class as the bluefish. Frank claims that the only mullet he ever tried to eat tasted like mud. He attributed this to his "damyankee tastes." But he's got a lot of rebel company, a lot of guys who claim that the only use for mullet should be as fish bait. I'm sure that none of them ever chewed down on a real fresh piece of mullet, dressed and put into the pan before it stopped kicking.

While some fish keep better than others, the fresher any fish, the better it will taste. Most of the guides I've fished with on far Canadian lakes, won't begin keeping shore-lunch walleyes or trout until about an hour before lunchtime — depending of course on how well the fish are biting. I know anglers who carry small frying pans in their shoulder bags when they wade a trout stream, and fry the keepers for lunch. I've tried this. Trout are definitely much tastier that way, beyond comparison.

One of the most delicious fish meals I remember consisted of whiting, caught out of the surf off a southern beach. We had a cottage nearby. As we caught each whiting, we dressed it immediately in the surf and sent it with one of the kids to the kitchen, where it was mealed and dropped immediately into the frying pan. Before we sat down to eat, we thought we'd caught twice as many whiting as we needed. But we cleaned the platter and could have gone for more.

CLEANING

There are many ways to prepare fish for cooking. The cleaning usually depends on the fish species, size, local custom and other such factors. All fish must be scaled, skinned or filleted before they are further prepared for the stove or table. If you plan to keep a fish for a while before scaling and plan to cook your meat with the skin on, then the fish should be kept wet until scaling time. Otherwise the skin dries and anchors the scales in such a manner that they are difficult to dislodge.

You can scale a fish with your knife blade, but most fish knives have dull, serrated edges on top of the blade for this purpose. There are other types of fish scalers on the market also. All are effective in dislodging the scales if you scrape from the tail toward the head. A few guys I know gut and eat their small eight- to ten-inch stream trout without bothering to scale them. These fish have very small scales, easily removed, and to me the trout taste better scaled.

Naturally the size of a fish and how you cut it up, or whether you cut it up at all, depends on how you plan to prepare it for eating. Small fish may be cooked whole or split to fit the pan you have along. Large ones are often left whole for baking, or cut into edible chunks or flat pieces for broiling, or even sliced as vertical steaks, as is often done with a large salmon. No matter how you cut the meat, do not clip off the fins. All this does is leave jagged bones and ends of bones in the meat. If you cook the fish with the fins on, you can pull out each fin with its entire set of bones.

Those who clean a lot of fish will tell you that the easiest and most satisfactory way to prepare them for cooking is by filleting. Properly done, filleting wastes little meat, leaving only the skeleton with all those bones you'd rather not have stuck in your throat. In filleting, the skin is often left on the softer meated fish to hold it together for cooking. And there are those who maintain that the skin imparts the juices, and savor found under it, to the cooked meat. If you leave the skin on, then you must scale the fish before filleting.

A man with enough experience behind him can fillet a fish before you can get the scales off to dress it another way. I've watched guides who could do the job with a few quick strokes of the knife. With one stroke they cut behind the gill plate to the backbone, turn the knife blade parallel to backbone and, following it as closely as possible, cut off one side of the fish to the end of the meat at the tail. (You can feel the blade against the backbone.) Some guides take off a small front section of the rib case in this cut and trim it off later with a flat stroke of the knife.

A similar cut down the other side of the fish provides a second fillet with the skin on. If the fish has been scaled and the fillets planned in this manner, the job is done except for washing off blood and other matter. If the fish is firm-fleshed enough and you want the meat with no skin, turn the

HOW TO FILLET A FISH

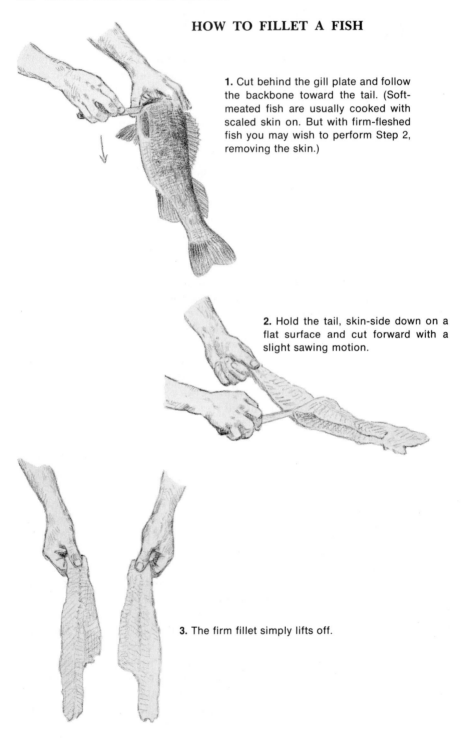

1. Cut behind the gill plate and follow the backbone toward the tail. (Soft-meated fish are usually cooked with scaled skin on. But with firm-fleshed fish you may wish to perform Step 2, removing the skin.)

2. Hold the tail, skin-side down on a flat surface and cut forward with a slight sawing motion.

3. The firm fillet simply lifts off.

fillet skin side-down on a dressing board or other flat surface; hold the very tip of the tail in your fingers; push your knife blade at a forward angle to the skin; and, holding the blade against the skin, cut forward with a slight sawing motion (still holding the tail) to cleanly separate flesh and skin for a pure chunk of meat.

The questions from that point are *How large do you like your fillets?* and *What you intend to do with them?* Fried, you may like fillets one size. Broiled, another. One of my fishing partners, Carter Jordan, likes to cut his fillets in strips about four or five inches long, and one half to 1-inch thick. Then he meals and fries them in deep hot fat. A fellow can't quite eat his weight in these, but he tries.

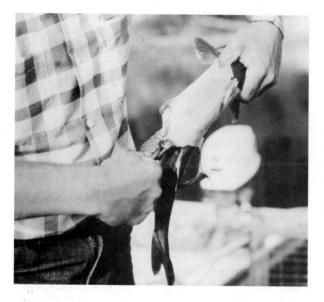

To skin a catfish, grip the head in one hand and cut around the skin behind the gills without cutting meat. Strip off the skin with dull nipper.

The catfish, highly prized for its meat, wears a thin but rather tough hide that must be peeled. A fellow who knows what tools to use, what cuts to make, and where to pull, can skin a catfish in seconds. Donald Spence, who was a commercial catfish dealer in Mississippi before he became a game warden, does the job as neatly and as quickly as anyone I've ever seen. Gripping the head in one hand, Don makes a cut all around the head behind the gills and just deep enough to separate the skin without cutting into the meat. With a pair of dull nipper pliers that won't bite through the skin, Don picks up the loose skin and simply strips it off as though he were peeling a ripe peach.

I've seen catfish much too large to skin by holding their heads in the hand. But this problem is usually solved by nailing the head to a tree and working off the skin with nippers.

COOKING

Most fish are edible if the cook knows how to prepare them. Some are better than others, naturally, but we pass up a good many varieties either because we can get those that taste better to us, or for other reasons. A jackfish — or pickerel, if you want to be technical — is loaded with small bones but carries some of the sweetest meat of any fresh water fish. The trick is to make narrow, vertical cuts in the meat to sever the bones and allow the hot grease to get to them. Some cooks help this process of dissolving the bones by marinating the pieces in a solution of vinegar and lemon juice.

Another fish that's full of fine bones is the sea-run white shad, a prized American delicacy. Broiled, it is delicious, but normally you must watch for those tiny bones throughout the meat. Daisy Oliver, wife of Captain A. P. Oliver, a famous St. Johns River (Florida) fishing guide, solves this problem with her own recipe that I've never seen used on shad anywhere else, but which might go well on pickerel and other bony fish.

After cleaning, Daisy cooks her shad whole. She puts it in a hot oven and turns it to brown on both sides. Then she pours a cup of lemon and orange juice in the bottom of the pan, turns the oven down to slightly over warm, and cooks her fish from six to eight hours. The shad is a fat fish and makes its own grease. Whether it's the long cooking or citrus juices or a combination. I have no idea, but the shad that Daisy cooks can be sliced with a cake knife. The bones are as soft as those in a can of salmon. Pressure cooking the fish, as it's done in a canning factory, would no doubt bring the same results.

The redhorse sucker is another species that most lovers of fish flesh pass up because of its bones. However, a lot of anglers I know in middle Tennessee are fond of suckers. They'll tell you right quick that as far as suckers are concerned, such swimmers as trout, bass and bream are the "trash" species. When the redhorses start "making mud" on their spawning runs up the fast water creeks and smaller rivers, word gets out. And everybody goes fishing. A man will close his filling station or drug store or stop his spring plowing to get to the creek. Letting a gang of hooks roll down the current to snag a female fanning out a bed in the gravel or snag a male there to service her spawn is an art as delicate as placing a trout fly in just the right spot.

It's what folks do with those suckers after they catch them that intrigues me as much as anything else. The suckers are cooked over a slow fire in tomato sauce. I had to agree, when I got myself wrapped around a generous helping, that they had a point about the "trash fish."

Many people do not bother with bluegills, called bream in many areas, and other small sunfish because cleaning them hardly seems worth the effort, even though the meat is sweet and delicious. An old swamper first showed me how he made light work of cleaning a bream. With a few licks of the back of his knife he knocked off the scales from the bream's back and upper half of its sides. Then he chopped it in two in a straight line from the back of the head to the vent, leaving as discards the gills and most of the guts. Amazingly enough, most of the edible part of the bream still remained, and the old swamper had made only a few passes at it.

Did you ever try to eat a grindle, bowfin, mudfish, cypress trout, dogfish, or fresh water ling? The same fish goes by all those names and possibly more. This fish is fairly common in the sluggish waters of the eastern part of the country. He puts up a jumping fight worthy of an old largemouth. When you think he's whipped, he'll come in twisting like an alligator in an effort to knot and break your line. Unfortunately, he is generally considered unfit for consumption. I tried to eat one that had been cleaned and cooked like any other fish. It had a good taste, but the bite I put in my mouth expanded as I chewed on it and turned into something that felt like a wad of wet cotton. When I wrote about that, I got a note from a riverman friend, "writ by hand" on lined tablet paper, explaining that I was all wet. The riverman claimed that a mudfish was good eating if, as soon it is landed, you hang it by the tail. Then you cut its throat and bleed it like a hog. Since then several other people have given me the same information. One of these days I'll try this technique.

OUTDOOR COOKERY

There are more ways to cook fish than perhaps any other kind of meat. And often, the way a fish is subjected to the fire depends on the fish itself and the circumstances. This is by no means a cookbook chapter, but I'd like to describe some of the unusual outdoor methods.

The shore lunch, for instance, is a delightful highlight of any all-day fishing trip. Most experienced guides from Florida, to Maine, to the far northwest Canadian lakes are adept at cooking. The procedure generally follows about the same routine. Around noon hour, the boats meet at some prearranged spot on a lake or river. The fishermen get out and walk around to stretch their legs and partake of a small libation while the guides build a fire and fillet the fish.

Most of the fish at these noon cookouts get the frying pan treatment. But some outdoor chefs are better than others. On one of these northwoods treks, the food was delicious. But along about four in the afternoon, my stomach felt as though I had swallowed a cup of carbolic acid. The second day I watched the food preparation more closely. The guides were letting their fires burn down and soaking rather than frying the fillets in half-hot hog lard.

One of my partners and I took over the cooking the next day. From the lodge we brought a roll of aluminum foil, potatoes, onions and a half pound of bacon. While the guides built a fire and cleaned the fish, we cut the potatoes and onions into slices about a half-inch thick. With two slices of

The fish, above left, were gutted and slipped onto spits. Then they were tied in place with fishing line. Above right, Woody Wheaton broils salmon with the aid of a mesh wire grill. Downwind of the drying racks in the photo below may not be the most pleasant place to stand, but this method of preserving fish provides essential winter store for Eskimos and their dogs.

potatoes as the bottom layer on a square of aluminum foil, a thick fillet topped by a bacon strip, and a layer of sliced onions, we rolled the aluminum into a packet about eight inches long, sealed it tightly, and put it on the fire for ten or twelve minutes on a side. A couple of times we opened and checked one of the parcels to keep them from over-cooking. The juices of the potatoes and onions steamed the fillet and the bacon gave it just the right touch of flavor. The next morning when the guides met us at the dock, they'd left their frying pans in camp and brought the aluminum foil.

At another Canadian camp, we had no foil. After the first day out, we scaled and gutted our lake trout, put them on a spit and tied them in place with a few half hitches of monofilament line. Then we roasted our fish over the coals – the way some of our cave ancestors must have done, minus the monofilament.

Woody Wheaton, the famous guide at Wheaton's Lodge on East Grand Lake in Maine, broils his shore lunch salmon steaks over a fire, but he does it with a long-handled mesh wire grill that hold several fillets at a time. Then Woody stands the grill beside the flames or props it over the coals. The mesh grill is much more maneuverable than a spit. One of Woody's noon cookouts is an event to remember.

I've never had to go back to the primitive method of baking fish in mud, but did it once as an experiment. Making up two plaques of mud about the size of a platter is messy business, and laying a good fish between them looks like sacrilege. But when the mud cooks hard and you split open the two pieces with your Boy Scout hand ax, you'll find good eating inside. We cooked our fish in white clay. I'm sure the red kind would have been as good. I have my doubts about some of the other mud types, such as gumbo.

The way fish is prepared usually depends on the number of mouths to feed as well as the kind of fish. There is quite an assortment of fish at an old southern fish fry, where anglers get together and pool their catches. The cooking container here may be an old iron wash pot that will hold a few gallons of shortening. A fire is built around the pot and the grease is declared hot enough when you spit in it and it spits back at you. More sanitary individuals usually throw in a few drops of water that pop like small firecrackers. The mealed fish pieces are dropped in, and these uncooked pieces go to the bottom of the pot. When they are exactly ready for eating, they obligingly rise to the top. Then they are forked out and laid on paper towels to drain. The shortening is so hot that apparently the meat absorbs none of it. The large cooking container turns out fried chunks of fish about as fast as the assembled gourmets can do away with them.

PRESERVING THE MEAT

But no matter what size your fish-eating crowd may be, you cannot always manage to do away with all the fish you catch. Often you will want to save some of that polyunsaturated flesh for future use. Today there are many methods of preserving fish. On our own continent the methods range from the most primitive to ultra-modern.

Drying

All along the Arctic coast from Hudson Bay to the Aleutian Islands, you will find racks of gilled and gutted fish drying in the sun, hopefully as a winter supply for both the natives and their dogs. These fish are taken generally from the runs of salmon, char and other anadromous species, and apparently they cure out successfully. But I have found that the downwind side of the racks is not always the most pleasant place to photograph or study them. As far as I know, I've never eaten a meal of fish preserved in this manner. They must be edible enough, for they have kept a vast population of Eskimos and Indians alive over the centuries. I am told that the natives usually select the fat fish with broad backs and hanging bellies for their own use and feed the leaner ones to their dogs.

Salting

In more ancient times, salting was done extensively. It remains applicable to this day. I can't say I was raised on salt mackerel, but when I was growing up, we got a tubful of it occasionally and spread it over a series of breakfasts. We considered mackerel a delicacy, and I still do, even with fresh fish available. Mackerel is treated both with dry salt and in brine. Once treated either way, it's a bit of trouble to prepare the fish for cooking. The fish must be soaked in fresh water overnight or longer to sweeten them enough for eating, but for some of us this is well worth the effort. Salt mackerel and other salt-treated fish are available in modern market places.

Freezing

With freezing plants, lockers and home units, more fish is preserved by freezing than by any other method. Most of it is dressed out and cut up in pieces ready for cooking as soon as thawed. If you plan to eat the fish within a few weeks of freezing, then wrapping in regular freezer paper is adequate. If we think we'll keep fish much longer than that, we pack the cut pieces in cartons, fill them to the top with water and freeze. This treatment keeps them fresh for long periods.

Smoking

People smoke fish either because they have no other way to preserve it, or because they like the smoked flavor. Many consider smoked fish a gourmet snack. I have been in situations when smoking was our only method of saving a fine catch, or when we wanted to pack home a few fish. In at least a few of these instances, we found it necessary to improvise our smokers out of primitive materials.

Once on a late fall big-game at Bridger Lake south of Yellowstone Park in the far northwest corner of Wyoming, we found big cutthroat trout, up to six pounds and larger, congregated in the holes of Yellowstone River that flows in a wide sweep around one end of the lake. Someone had said that at this time of year the fish migrated out of the creeks and shallow headwaters which were likely to freeze almost solid during the winter months. Whatever the trout were doing, their appetites were not reduced. We had packed in our fishing gear and had no trouble catching as many of the big trout as we wanted. This added immeasurably to the excitement of our hunt and to the pleasure over our camp fare as well. Max Wilde, our outfitter on this and many such trips into the Thorofare and the country around it, suggested that we might like to smoke a few of those cutthroats to take home with us.

We set up our smoker near the camp but far enough from the tents to keep down a danger of fire. We were making no attempt to go completely primitive and create a rig out of such materials as earth, rock and tree bark, as is sometimes done by the pure in heart. It was simpler for us to give a few concessions to civilization.

As I remember, we selected a bank with a slight slope, dug a fire pit to mineral soil and made a sort of fire box out of flat slide rock. From the stone box we extended two lengths of stove pipe uphill at an angle to the bottom of a log frame made by driving four birch posts into the ground and tacking in an upper and lower platform of small, slender poles, an inch or more apart. Our cover was a piece of tarp, wrapped in such a way around the frame as to leave a small vent in the top.

We filleted our fish into thin slices. Most recipes call for soaking them overnight in brine to harden the flesh and then washing them in fresh water before smoking. We did no more than wash our fillets to get out all blood. Then we dried, salted, and peppered them for eating before laying them on the pole racks.

I'm sure the job could have been done more quickly. But for two days of daylight hours we kept the interior of the canvas-covered frame saturated with smoke from the green aspen wood. We turned and rearranged the fillets a few times to give them full advantage of the smoke. The guides considered our fish fully smoked when they were brown and firm, but not yet hard enough to be on the tough side. I heartily agreed that the smoking was right when I bit into a chunk of that meat.

Many outdoorsmen make home smokers out of a variety of objects, most popular of which seems to be a metal drum with a fire box in the bottom, a grill near the top with a metal baffle just under it, and a loose lid which can be propped open or otherwise regulated to control the draft.

Another favorite home smoker is an old refrigerator shell, which usually contains the grill shelves. The hull is converted to allow a controlled flow of air into the bottom and out through a vent on top. The top vent is often made with a short section of 1- or 2-inch water pipe.

People who are refrigerator smokers do it the easy way, with a 110 or 120 volts and an old electric burner, which they keep at the proper heat level and covered with enough green hickory or other sweet wood sawdust or chips to give the proper amount of smoke without flames.

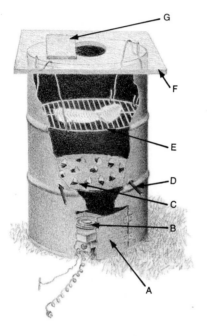

55-GALLON DRUM SMOKER

Components include **(A)** a hinged fire door, cold-chiseled from the drum wall, **(B)** an electric hot plate that smolders sweet-wood sawdust or chips, **(C)** a baffle, cold-chiseled from the drum lid and perforated with a dozen good-sized chisel holes, **(D)** baffle support rods inserted parallel through holes cold-chiseled through the drum sides, **(E)** a regular charcoal broiler grill suspended by heavy wire, **(F)** a plywood cover with a four-inch hole in the center, **(G)** a board that regulates draft. (An additional grill could be suspended above the first to handle more meat.)

TROPHY CONSIDERATIONS

Almost any taxidermist can give you an idea of the value most fishermen place on game fish trophies. Some of the local pros—those lads to whom taxidermy is a home hobby—say that fish mounts make up a good percentage of their business. I can name a few big commercial shops devoted almost exclusively to fish.

Fish are preserved as trophies for a number of reasons. Perhaps the main reason is size. A fellow may go along year after year catching small black bass. He may never have taken one over five pounds in all of his days. Suddenly one afternoon about dusk he ties into a twelve-pounder and lands it. It's scarcely larger than half the size of the world record. But as far as this fisherman is concerned, there is no better record anywhere.

Then too, many fish are mounted because they are of a species the angler regards as unusual. For example, a fellow may have read and dreamed about catching a muskellunge. The fellow finally has the time or is financially able to make the trip to distant musky waters. Or a native fisherman of musky country may have tried long for a creditable representative of these unpredictable fish. Regardless of the weight, a long-sought musky may put up a savage battle and must go on the den wall.

A fish may be preserved as evidence of the trip of a lifetime, or an unforgettable experience to some far wilderness or corner of the oceanic world. I have on my den wall an arctic char taken out of Tree River, which flows into Coronation Bay off the Arctic Ocean. It's not the only char I ever took. Nor is Tree River the only place where I've caught char. But at 21 pounds, this one is my largest. But the real reason I got the fish mounted was for its spectacular coloration and the memories I knew it would help me hold of that distant, lonely land. I must admit that since few anglers around my part of the world ever saw an arctic char, the trophy is a good conversation piece. When one of my visitors asks questions about it, he doesn't have to twist my pectoral fin to get the story. Most of these visitors have seen sheep, elk, caribou, bear and other trophies such as I have around, but the char is something new to them.

LANDING AND CARE OF A TROPHY

Landing a fish you think you may want for a trophy should require a bit more care than you provide when fishing for meat. Netting seems to be the accepted practice for fresh water fish. But most experienced salt-water anglers I know prefer the gaff. The net does little to damage the skin of a fish, and the old guide knows when and where to use his gaff. One of the common faults is bringing in a fish that's too "green." The idea is to play it down until it's so exhausted that it can't damage its skin or fins in the bottom of a boat or on a rocky beach. I've seen only one big "green" fish, a marlin, gaffed and brought aboard while it was still full enough of fight to take the place apart. We were lucky that someone didn't get hurt.

Some anglers for the smaller varieties prefer to play down their fish to a point where it can be lifted out of the water by hand. There are several dangers to this. You can grip a black bass by the lower jaw and paralyze it, but you'd better not try putting your fingers in the mouth of a pike or walleye. You can pick up a walleye by the gill plate, but the razor-sharp gill of a snook will slice and make a frightful wound.

Even an experienced guide will sometimes make mistakes. I was fishing in Florida's Mosquito Lagoon with a guide who'd done nothing but fish all his life. We were after the tremendous spotted weakfish that hang out there, but we couldn't catch anything but small ones when we used artificials. When we went to pinfish bait, the first strike the guide had was from a big catfish. Disgusted, the guide held it over the side of the boat and tried to knock if off the hook with his heavy pliers. The fish, lightly hooked, flopped off. But instead of falling into the water, it flipped back into the boat and fell on its back. Its sharp dorsal fin stuck in the top of the guide's bare foot. Almost before we pulled the fin out, the foot was swelling. So we cranked up and made for the dock. The poor guy couldn't walk for several days. This experience only convinced me further that any angler should be careful when he fools around with the fins or head of a fish.

After you have subdued it, a fish requires special handling if you plan to save it as a trophy. One of my favorite and most informed outdoor partners is Frank Woolner. Frank is editor of *The Saltwater Sportsman* and author of a number of charming outdoor books. He gave us a valuable tip on how a trophy fish should be treated between the hook and the taxidermist.

"A fish to be mounted," he said, "should be handled with loving care from the moment of capture. A striped bass, for example, should be iced belly *up*. Otherwise blood may flow into and stain the white belly scales. Never pile other fish on top of a trophy specimen. This dents it and causes a more rapid softening."

THE NATURAL LOOK

Both Frank Woolner and Jim Gay suggest that the first thing an angler should do after landing a fish is to take a close-up color photograph if possible. The color photo is more important for the highly colored than it is for the drab fishes. Most fish lose their color quickly after they die. Time after time I've caught arctic grayling that flashed a beautiful purple and gold when they fought my hook in the water. After they were landed and lifeless for a few minutes, they had changed to a dull metallic gray. After the color change, I wouldn't have recognized them as the same species except for the high spread of the dorsal fin.

The color of many individual fish reflects the water in which they live. A rainbow trout in a shallow, sunlit stream is a splash of color. One that spends its days at forty to sixty feet or deeper in a mountain lake is usually clothed in silvery sheen like a steelhead. A largemouth bass comes in colors that range from greenish to almost black, depending on its habitat. A color photo of your fish will help insure that the mounted version will look like the fresh caught specimen.

Woolner offers a further word of advice on this. "When you can, you should give your fish to a taxidermist who is a native of the fish's locale, because he'll know the subtleties of color. Therefore, take your tropical specimens to a tropical taxidermist, and choose a northern expert when you have a northern fish."

Your next problem is to get your fish to the taxidermist in as good condition as possible. The chances are that within hours you can have it in a freezer. And frozen is the way the man who will mount your trophy prefers to get it. He can preserve it in this manner until he gets around to your job.

Woolner suggests that for freezing the fish should be wrapped in smooth plastic, placed in the deep freezer—belly up with nothing else laid on top, or at least not until the carcass is hard as a rock. The fish should be delivered to your taxidermist either by hand or by air freight if the distance warrants.

There seems to be a difference of opinion, even among the experts, as to how a trophy should be mounted. Some favor using the actual skin of the fish. Others say that the skin will deteriorate in short order and that the best method is to make a mold out of molding plaster and take an impression of the body, fins and all.

Depending on the taxidermist, any one of a number of materials may be used to make a cast, which is then painted and mounted on a board. This then is supposed to represent your fish. This type of trophy preparation comes in varying degrees of excellence, though I must admit that some of those I've seen look as though they were just porcelain purchased at the nearest novelty shop.

Maybe I'm old-fashioned, but the few fish I've had mounted are in their natural covering and seem to have held up extremely well. You may be certain that I inquired ahead of time to learn how my chosen taxidermist planned to preserve my trophy.

Modern transportation and ultra-modern conveniences being what they are, possibly only one out of a thousand fish is ever delivered other than fresh or frozen to the taxidermist. But there will always continue to be that exception.

MY BIG GRINDLE

The only fish I ever had mounted that wasn't fresh or frozen when delivered was an old grindle caught in the heart of the Okefenokee Swamp. We'd been camped for two weeks on a pole platform built just above the surface of the water, at least one day of paddling away from the nearest landing. In those days around the swamp there were few roads—only two-track sandy trails. By boat, foot and car, we were two or three days away from the nearest refrigeration.

I caught a grindle that went over twelve pounds, and that was a big one, even then. Since I had the urge to save that fish as a trophy, the only way I could preserve the hide was to skin it out. Being inexperienced, I gave the job a day of my fishing time. But having skinned innumerable birds and animals, I at least knew the basics.

I carefully removed the gills. Then I made an incision from the top of the head above the gill cover, around the outside of the cover and in front of the pectoral fin to the jaw. Then I cut from the gill plate along the lateral line to the base of the caudal fin (tail fin), being careful to pick up the skin with my knife blade and slit just under it. After that it was a relatively simple matter to peel the hide off the flesh, skin around the fin bones until I could lift them out, cut through the tailbone without damaging the hide on the other side and then carefully work out the eyes, brain and all fleshy parts around the head.

When I had removed all flesh possible, I liberally salted down my hide and rolled it up. A week or so later when I was at Silver Springs, Florida, I showed my grindle hide to Ross Allen, the famous naturalist and herpetologist. And Ross offered to mount the fish for me.

I found out later that I'd made at least one sizeable mistake, that of leaving the scales on that old grindle. As the hide dried the scales curled up into a frizzled pattern and every scale locked itself into the skin. Ross said that removing the scales was mostly a matter of prying them out one at the time.

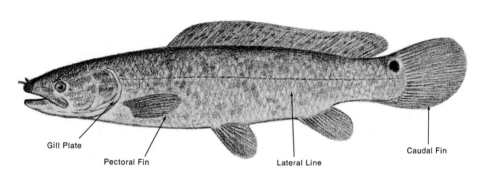

Gill Plate

Pectoral Fin

Lateral Line

Caudal Fin

Also called bowfin, dogfish, mudfish, or scaled ling, the grindle is a still-water fish with poor-eating, pasty flesh. It puts up a good fight though, and big ones, like the author's, provide the makings for creditable mounts.

HOW TO SKIN A TROPHY

For more specific and complete instructions on taking the hide off any fish, I went as usual to Jim Gay. Here is what Jim told me:

"My experience in fish mounting has been mostly with trout, and I'm for the skinning method. First, to cast and make a replica in plaster, plastic or whatever, we need to have a perfectly firm, fresh fish to cast. But there are going to be times in any sportsman's life (hopefully) when he is in the boondocks. Then the only way to save the trophy fish is to skin it yourself.

"First, take pictures. Then make an outline drawing by laying the fish on its side on a piece of paper, paper sack flattened out, newspaper, birch bark, or whatever you are ingenious enough to come up with. Then draw as accurate an outline as you can. Next draw another from the top view, first laying the fish on its belly. You'll have to hold him up with one hand and draw around with the other. These drawings help the taxidermist make a 'body' on which the skin will fit tightly. With the drawing as guidance the taxidermist can re-create your fish from the skin alone. He can do a real top job with the photos and drawings. (See pages 142 and 143.)

"Find a clean, flat place to do the skinning, such as a board, a flat rock, a boat seat or the bottom of an overturned boat. Make the opening on the side that will be next to the wall when you hang your fish as a trophy. Don't whack into the belly! Usually the cut is made along the lateral line from tail to gill opening. Skin carefully, tenderly, because I'd want the scales all left on. On a trout these are very small or fine, but missing ones will show up in the finished mount when the actual skin is used. Where the fin bones go into the body, scissors are handy to cut them, but a sharp knife will do it. Be careful.

"The head or skull is the most difficult. I usually sever it from the body at the top of the gill opening. I don't cut the skin, though. This severing is done from the inside as you skin out the body. Then the body skin can be cased over the skull as is done with birds and animals, only you leave the jaw bones in, similar to the way you leave the bill or beak of a bird attached to the skull. But with a fish you do not keep the skull, only the upper and lower maxillaries, or jaw bones. Then as with any skinning, cut off all gobs of fat or meat.

"As with all skins, salt is the best preservative. But if for any reason you don't have salt, air-dry the skin with a little smoking over a 'cold' fire, as the early mountain man did with his skins."

The chances are slim that in these modern days you might get caught in the far back country, as I was in the Okefenokee Swamp, with a trophy fish you'd like to keep. If and when you think there's such a possibility on your next trip, your best bet will be to go to your taxidermist before you start out. He'll give you all the information which will enable you to do a bang-up skinning and skin preserving job.

Knowing what to do is well worth the time it takes to learn.

SKINNING FOR A MOUNT

1. Take color pictures from different angles.

2. Make outline drawings from side and top views.

3. On the side that will be mounted against the wall, cut the fish open. Don't whack into the belly!

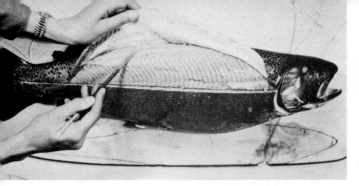

4. Skin carefully, tenderly. Try not to knock off any scales.

5. Cut the fins off with a scissors or sharp knife.

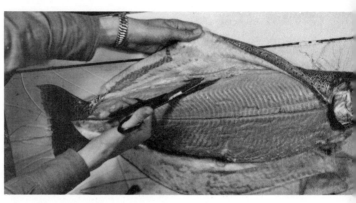

6. To separate the head from the body, cut free the lower gill area but only bend back the top, removing flesh inside the head without cutting the connecting skin.

7. Remove the skull but leave the lower jaw bones. Then flesh off all meat and fat. Salt everything liberally.

Photo Credits

The author made all photos with the exception of those listed below:

Eric Blair/Outdoors Associates: page 2
Bill McRae: pages 9, 12 (top), 14 (top left)
Leonard Lee Rue III: pages 11, 14 (top right and both on bottom), 107, 112
Wyoming Game & Fish Commission: page 8

Index